THE TRINITY OF SIN

This book is dedicated to my uncle, Rev. Dawuda Som, who nurtured my spiritual growth in early childhood and laid a good foundation of the Christian faith.

THE TRINITY OF SIN

Yusufu Turaki

Copyright © 2012 by Yusufu Turaki

Published 2011 by **HippoBooks**, an imprint of WordAlive, ACTS, Challenge Enterprises and Zondervan.

WordAlive Publishers, PO Box 4547, GP0-00100 Nairobi, Kenya
www.wordalivepublishers.org

Africa Christian Textbooks (ACTS), TCNN, PMB 2020, Bukuru 930008, Plateau State, Nigeria
www.africachristiantextbooks.com

Challenge Enterprises of Ghana, PO Box 5723, Accra, Ghana
www.ceghana.com

Zondervan, Grand Rapids, Michigan 49530
www.zondervan.com

Library of Congress Cataloging-in-Publication Data
Turaki, Yusufu, 1946-
    The trinity of sin / Yusufu Turaki.
       p. cm.
    Includes bibliographical references (p. 187–190).
    ISBN 978-9966-003-18-8 (softcover)
    1. Sin—Christianity. 2. Theology—Africa. 3. God (Christianity) 4. Jesus Christ—Crucifixion. I. Title.
BT715.T87 2011
241'.3—dc23   2011044328

All rights reserved. No part of this book may be reproduced or transmitted in any form or by any means, electronic or mechanical, including photocopying, recording or by any information storage or retrieval system without permission in writing from the publisher.

All Scripture quotations, unless otherwise indicated, are taken from The Holy Bible: *New International Version*®. NIV®. Copyright © 1973, 1978, 1984, 2011 by Biblica, Inc.™ Used by permission. All rights reserved worldwide.

Cover design: projectluz.com
Book design: To a Tee Ltd, www.2at.com

12 13 14 15 16 17 18 /DCI/ 19 18 17 16 15 14 13 12 11 10 9 8 7 6 5 4 3 2 1

CONTENTS

Preface xiii

1. **Introduction** 1
   My Interest in Sin 1
   Structure of the Book 4

PART I: THEOLOGICAL BACKGROUND

2. **Traditional African Beliefs** 9
   Fundamental Theological Beliefs 10
      Belief in impersonal powers 10
      Belief in spirit beings 11
      Belief in many divinities 12
      Belief in a Supreme Being 13
      Belief in a hierarchy of spiritual beings 13
   Fundamental Psychological Beliefs 14
   Fundamental Philosophical Beliefs 15
      Holism 16
      Spiritualism 17
      Dynamism 18
      Communalism 19
      Fatalism 21
   Fundamental Moral and Ethical Beliefs 21
      Law of harmony 22
      Law of the spirit 22
      Law of power 23
      Law of kinship 24
   Summary 24

3. God and Sin 25

God's Nature 26
- God is a Trinity 27
- God is sovereign 28
- God is eternal 28
- God is the eternal Word 29
- God is eternal spirit 29
- God is good 30
- God is wise 30
- God is holy 31
- God is righteous 32
- God is just 32
- God is angry 33
- God is true 33
- God is faithful 34

God's Laws 35
- God's universal physical laws 35
- God's universal moral laws 35

Why a Right Understanding of God Matters 36

4. Creation: Good or Bad? 37

The View of World Religions 37

The View of African Religions 38

The Christian View 39

Why a Right Understanding of Creation Matters 41

5. Evil, Sin and Free Will 42

The Nature of Evil 43

Evil and Free Will 43

Why We Were Created 44

Our Original Condition 45

God's First Covenant with Adam and Eve 46

What Happened in Eden 47
- Who was Satan? 47
- What was the temptation? 47

    The Fall and God's Second Covenant with Adam and Eve 49

    Why Understanding Free Will Matters 50

6. The Power of Temptation 52

    The Power of Temptation 53

    The Context of Temptation 54

    The Instrument of Temptation 54

    Rebellion and Disobedience 54

    The Consequences of the Fall 56

        Inherited guilt 58

        Inherited corruption 59

    God's Judgement and Punishment 59

        God's judgement on the serpent 60

        God's judgement on Eve 60

        God's judgement on Adam 61

        Living in exile 62

    Conclusion 62

7. Human Nature 64

    Traditional African View of Human Nature 64

    Biblical View of Human Nature 67

    Spirit, Soul and Body 67

        Sin and the spirit 69

        Sin and the soul 71

        Sin and the body 73

    Conclusion 74

PART II: THE TRINITY OF SIN

8. **Self-centredness and Pride** 77
   Defining Pride 77
   The Sin of Pride in Satan 79
   Pride and the Fall 79
   Self and Sin 81
       Heart and sin 82
       Flesh and sin 84
   Sins Related to Self-Centredness and Pride 85
   Dealing with the Sins of Self-Centredness and Pride 87
   Summary 87

9. **Greed and Lust** 89
   Defining Greed and Lust 89
   Greed, Lust and the Fall 90
       Greed 91
       Lust 91
   Self-centredness and Pride and Greed and Lust 92
   Sins Related to Greed and Lust 92
   Dealing with the Sins of Greed and Lust 93

10. **Anxiety and Fear** 95
    Anxiety, Fear and the Fall 95
    Defining Anxiety and Fear 97
    Self-Centredness and Pride, Greed and Lust and Anxiety and Fear
       98
    Sins Related to Anxiety and Fear 98
    Dealing with the Sins of Anxiety and Fear 101

PART III: GOD'S SOLUTION TO THE PROBLEM OF SIN

11. Redemption in Jesus Christ 105
The Cross: God's Response to the Fall 106
Adam and the Second Adam 108
God's Plan of Salvation and Redemption 109
All believers are chosen by the Father 109
All believers are redeemed by the Son 110
All believers are sealed by the Spirit 111
Christ's Work of Reconciliation 112
The Resurrection Power of Jesus 113
The Church, the Body of Christ 114

12. Applying the Power of the Cross of Christ 117
Sins and Sin 117
Sins and personal guilt 118
Sin and inherited corruption 119
Spiritual Death and Resurrection 121
Spiritual Death and Remarriage 123
Conclusion 124

13. Self-Centredness, Pride and the Cross 125
Dealing with the Self 125
Denying ourselves 125
Mortifying the flesh 126
Dealing with Pride 127
Confessing our pride 127
Becoming a servant 128
Imitating Christ 128
Summary 129

14. Greed, Lust and the Cross ... 131

The Holy Spirit and Regeneration ... 132
- Regeneration and faith ... 132
- Regeneration and new life ... 133
- Regeneration and eternal life ... 134

Nurturing New Life ... 134
- Greed and the bread of life ... 135
- Greed and living water ... 135
- Lust and the light of the world ... 136
- Putting off the works of the flesh ... 137

Sanctification and Putting on Christ ... 138

Walking in the Spirit ... 139

Summary ... 140

15. Anxiety, Fear and the Cross ... 141

Realization of Our Creaturehood ... 141

Restoration and Reconciliation in the Cross of Christ ... 143

God's Sovereignty ... 144

Worship of God ... 146

The Resurrection Power of Jesus ... 147

Jesus' Teachings on Worry ... 148

Summary ... 149

PART IV: SIN ISSUES IN MODERN AFRICA

16. Spiritual Idolatry in Modern Africa 153

    An African Ancestor in the Garden of Eden 154

    Western Neopagan Spirituality 154

    Idolatry 156

    Syncretism 159

    Examples of Modern Spiritual Idolatry in Africa 160
        Quest for spiritual and mystical power 162
        Quest for life force and spiritual powers 163
        Quest to control the spirit world 164
        Quest to communicate with the spirit world 165
        Quest to maintain harmony with the spirit world 166
        Observance of taboos 167
        Consultation of African Specialists 168
        Joining secret cults 168

    Spiritual Powers and Warfare 168

17. Social and Communal Sins in Africa 170

    Foundations of Attitudes, Behaviour and Social Practice 170

    Kinship and Communal Morality 173
        The place of outsiders and strangers 174
        Biblical teachings on outsiders and strangers 175

    Sin, Shame and Guilt in Africa 176

    Creating a Just, Participatory and Sustainable Society 179
        Sustainability 181
        Justice 181
        Participation 182
        Application to Africa 183

    Summary 184

18. Conclusion 186

    BIBLIOGRAPHY 187

    NOTES 191

PREFACE

Many African Christians cannot explain what sin is, how it affects humans and society, or how it came into the world. The best they can offer is a mix of popular opinions, traditional views and guesswork that falls far short of what Scripture teaches. Their confusion leaves them powerless to deal with sin and live a victorious Christian life.

My goal in writing this book is to address this confusion. Drawing on my understanding of Africa's traditional beliefs and social and spiritual values, I will explain the scriptural teaching about sin and God's solution to it in terms that make sense to Africans.

Take the issue of who is primarily responsible for bringing sin into the world. Some Africans blame humans. Some blame Satan. Some blame evil spirits and supernatural powers. Some even blame God. Confusion reigns. Yet the answer to this question is very important. If we know how sin first came into the world, we will have a better idea of how to deal with it.

Or think about the mystery of where sin comes from. Does it come from within us, or is it some outside spiritual power that attacks us? When we do not understand its nature we cannot respond to it. If we cannot diagnose a disease, we cannot prescribe the right medicine.

Ignorant of what the Bible teaches about sin, many Africans resort to traditional practices to deal with sin in their lives and communities and fail to distinguish between the works of sin and the works of demons. They try to exorcise sin because they see it as something to be cast out, not something to be put to death through the cross of Christ. Instead of recognizing that sin is rooted in our characters, they interpret it as demonic possession, occupation by an external being. The Western response to this is to deny the power of the demonic, but there can be no doubt that demons do exert a powerful influence – but only where sin has given them a foothold. Once that sin is dealt with and removed, demons usually lose their influence.

Other Africans look for help in human philosophy or psychology. They interpret sinful attitudes, behaviours and practices as merely a matter of heredity or biology. And to a certain extent, they are right. A tendency to certain sins may run in a family, community, ethnic group or nation. Sin is spiritual and it exerts spiritual influence over individuals who live within a sinful environment. But sin is not simply hereditary; it also involves free will and choices. We cannot argue that because our stealing is hereditary we have no need to confess it is wrong.

In this book I will explain the origin and roots of sin; how it manifests itself in human nature; how it affects our behaviour, our communities and the world; God's solution to the problem of sin; and how to apply the power of the cross and blood of Jesus Christ to the works of sin and flesh in the lives of believers, communities and the world.

These issues have been much discussed in classical theology and philosophy. But we will not be considering those ideas here. Rather, my desire is to present a scriptural explanation of the origin, nature, effects and power of sin in human nature and God's solution to the sin problem within an African context.

In doing this, I will not be content to discuss sin only in general terms. That would be like describing a tree in terms of only the leaves, branches and trunk, without bothering to mention the roots. Our understanding of sin must go beyond describing the individual sins we can see or feel and must also identify its deep and hidden roots in self-centredness and pride, greed and lust, and anxiety and fear. We will see how the cross of Christ and the persons of the Trinity work together to give victory over each root sin.

Yusufu Turaki
Jos, Plateau State, Nigeria
October 2011

1
INTRODUCTION

Some sinful habits seem not to go away, no matter how many times we confess them. This problem exists because we don't understand the impact, power and effect of sin in our life and lack biblical knowledge about how to apply the benefits of our redemption by Christ through the ministry of the Holy Spirit and the word of God. Some, like me, have been influenced by a cultural understanding of sin, others by false teachings or a lack of any teaching. Some of us struggle because we lump all sins together and have only one approach to dealing with them. Or we may fail to distinguish between our sinful acts, behaviour and attitudes on the one hand, and our inherently sinful nature on the other.

Before we look at these issues in depth, and at God's solution to them, as revealed in Scripture, I would like to explain how I developed an interest in the subject of sin. I think that many of you will identify with my experience.

My Interest in Sin

I began to be interested in the subject of sin when I was between five and seven years old. At that time my uncle, the Rev. Dawuda Som, introduced me to Jesus Christ and presented me with a very simple model of the Christian faith:

1. God is the creator of everything, including all human beings.
2. God is holy; he is without sin and never does wrong or make mistakes.

3. Human beings are all born sinners and do wrong.
4. God punishes those who do wrong by sending them into the lake of fire.
5. God forgives our wrongdoing and gives us eternal life if we believe in his Son Jesus Christ and confess and forsake sin.
6. Believers in Jesus must confess their wrongdoing every day.
7. Believers in Jesus Christ draw their strength and power from God through praying in Jesus' name, reading or hearing God's word, and being led by the power of the Holy Spirit.

This simple model laid the foundation of my Christian teaching, doctrine and theology, and has proved useful when I have been teaching young converts. But what gripped my mind as a child and a "baby" Christian was an overwhelming sense of the power of sin in my life. This realization drove me to confess my sins at the end of each day. I would review all that I had done, thought or said and ask God to forgive for all the wrongs I had committed.

But my childhood experience also led to doubts. I would see my friends who were still immersed in African Traditional Religion go off to a shrine clutching a chicken. On their return, I would see marks of blood on their forehead, hands, legs, chest and stomach. When I asked what this meant, they would say that the sacrifice of the chicken at the shrine had removed some wrongdoing, evil, sickness or bad omen. The blood on them would provide protection and ward off evil. I found myself asking, "Why don't Christians have an effective way to ward off sin? If sin is dangerous because it sends people to hell, why isn't there a permanent cure for it? Why am I still struggling with sin?"

My problem was that I was thinking about the Christian faith in the same terms as African Traditional Religion. I revered the word of God, the Holy Spirit and Jesus Christ as holy, but I expected the same sort of quick and magical response from God as from a witchdoctor or medicine man.

I have since discovered that I was not alone in thinking in those terms. Many Africans seek quick and easy answers in traditional religion. And Africans are not alone in this; people from other groups all around the world are no less eager for a magical solution to the problem of sin.

As I matured as a Christian, I learned that sin cannot be removed by a sacrifice or ritual or a ceremony at a shrine. Sin is not an external object or a disease that can be warded off. It is an enduring power within us. It has already captured our inner being. It has become our very nature. Sin is us and we are our sins.

Since Christianity did not have the rituals and ceremonies of African Traditional Religion, I had to accept the need for penitence, the habit of regular confession of sin to God. Nightly penitence became a ritual that moulded my moral and spiritual habits.

But as I gained still more knowledge and experience, I realized that penitence itself can become an attempt to earn righteousness and can become a hindrance to genuine spiritual growth. It is not penitence that grants victory over sin, but the application of Christ's redemption on the cross through the ministry of the Holy Spirit in our lives.

My struggle with sin intensified when I enrolled in a seminary. I worked hard to understand what the Holy Scriptures and Christian theology have to say about the nature, power and effects of sin in human life, and particularly in the lives of Christians. My motivation was not a desire for academic knowledge but the need to find victory over sin in my own life. I was aware that I had some sinful habits that did not go away, no matter how many times I confessed them.

I was like many of us, for whom sin takes centre stage in our life. Despite studying and even memorizing the word of God, we sin daily. Even though as Christians we have the Holy Spirit living in us, we still sin. Sin dominates and controls us. Once in a while, it embarrasses us when it pops up in public. But even if we keep our sin hidden from public scrutiny, we live with a sense of shame or guilt. We feel miserable and awkward. We know exactly what Paul was referring to in Romans 7 when he said that although he felt "delight in God's law" (Rom 7:22) he was still captive to the law of sin.[1]

Yet Paul also makes it clear that the battle to overcome sin does not have to be lost. He writes:

> Therefore, brothers and sisters, we have an obligation – but it is not to the flesh, to live according to it. For if you live according to the flesh, you will die; but if by the Spirit you put to death the misdeeds of the body, you will live. For those who

are led by the Spirit of God are the children of God. (Rom 8:12–14)

So why do so many of us Christians live under the power of sin and not live holy lives? Why do we not experience the power of the Holy Spirit and the word of God in our lives? Why do we not lead Christ-like lives?

My struggles with sin, like those of many African Christians, sprang from a shallow understanding of sin and a lack of proper biblical teaching. But over the years, my intensive study of the problem of sin and of victory has led me to biblical insights and meaningful answers. My goal in this book is to help Christians, especially African Christians, understand more about sin and learn how to overcome it through the cross of Christ, the ministry of the Holy Spirit and the word of God.

Structure of the Book

This book falls into four main parts.

Part I provides the broad theological context for the discussion by defining sin, and its origin, nature, power and effects in human life.

Chapter 2 describes the influence of the African world view on African theology in general and shows how this affects our understanding of the nature of sin and the appropriate response to it.

Chapter 3 deals with our understanding of the relationship between God and evil.

Chapter 4 shows how our understanding of creation affects our understanding of evil and sin.

Chapter 5 deals with the origin of evil, sin and temptation.

Chapter 6 deals with the power of temptation and the fall of Adam and Eve.

Chapter 7 deals with our understanding of human nature.

Part II describes three pairs of sins that lie at the root of all other sins. In discussing each pair, I define them, show their role in the original fall, and summarize the categories of sins that emanate from them.

Chapter 8 discusses self-centredness and pride.

Chapter 9 discusses greed and lust.
Chapter 10 discusses anxiety and fear.

Part III describes God's solution to human sinfulness and explains how we can learn to apply the power of the death and resurrection of Jesus Christ in our own lives. It will teach Christians how to solve their own sin problem and have victory over sin by living a Christ-like life.

Chapter 11 describes God's solution to the problem of sin through the work of Jesus Christ on the cross and the ministry of the Holy Spirit in regeneration and sanctification. It reminds us that this redemption is not automatic; it needs to be applied.

Chapter 12 contains suggestions on how to apply Christ's work to the sin in our lives.

Chapter 13 provides practical applications in regard to sins of self-centredness and pride.

Chapter 14 contains applications in relation to sins of greed and lust.

Chapter 15 contains applications in relation to sins of anxiety and fear.

Part IV deals with issues in modern Africa that Christians must address very seriously.

Chapter 16 looks at our broken relationship with our Creator, focusing on the spiritual idolatry that is rooted in our traditional religious background and world view.

Chapter 17 deals with our broken relationships with others, looking at social and communal sins that are rooted in traditional kinship and communal values.

I challenge every Christian to make every effort to learn more about the roots, origin, nature, power and effects of sin in one's life and in society. Secondly, I encourage every Christian to strive to win victory over sin. My prayer is that many will find this book helpful in their Christian walk.

PART I: THEOLOGICAL BACKGROUND

Before we can begin, we need to have a working definition of what sin is. In my language, Gyong, which is spoken in central Nigeria, there are three words for sin. *Yam* refers to committing an offence by touching something forbidden. In touching, one takes on the nature of the forbidden thing and becomes one with it. *Bithikyuye* refers to a general state of wickedness or badness while *chooky* means to go beyond the limits, to trespass or transgress.

Chooky comes closest to the Bible's understanding of sin as occurring "when a person deliberately or accidentally steps over the line of the law of God".[2] John, for example, says that "Everyone who sins breaks the law; in fact, sin is lawlessness" – 1 John 3:4. Sin can also be defined as falling short or missing the target, as in Romans 3:23 where Paul says that "All have sinned and fall short of the glory of God". This definition shows that we are all sinners, not just because of what we do but because we all fall short of the high moral and spiritual status God intended us to have.

African Christians sometimes struggle with the Christian concept of sin because of their background in traditional religion and the world view that flows from it. In saying this, I am not saying that our traditional background is entirely evil or unhelpful when it comes to understanding Christian spirituality. Like all cultures, African culture has both good and bad elements. Indeed, when it is renewed and transformed by the gospel of Christ and biblical teaching, our African background enables us to make a unique contribution to world Christianity. But when it comes to sin, traditional influences can lead to misunderstandings. Thus it is important to give a brief description of the key elements of African Traditional Religion and the associated world view so that we can better compare and contrast them with what the Bible teaches.

PART I: THEOLOGICAL BACKGROUND

2

TRADITIONAL AFRICAN BELIEFS

African Christians do not abandon all their traditional beliefs and culture when they become Christians. Nor should they. Christianity does not negate our Africanness but affirms it. There is much that is good in our heritage. But our Christian spirituality and practice are influenced by our Africanness to a far greater extent than we may realize.

What the Christian faith and biblical teachings do is give us a new compass to chart the course of our life within our African context. Yet a compass is of limited use unless we know where we are and where we want to go. Think of someone who is kidnapped and dumped somewhere in the bush. Which way should he go to find help? Should he head north or south, east or west? He has no way of knowing unless he has some understanding of where he is.

In the same way, African Christians are surrounded by the "bush" of African culture. It is pervasive. We want to move towards more biblical living, but we are not certain which direction to walk in because we do not know exactly where we are. We cannot simply follow the directions provided by someone from another culture, because he is starting from a different place. He may need to walk north to find help; we may need to head south. That is why it is important for African Christians who want to be authentic and relevant to have a thorough knowledge of the African terrain. Without it, we cannot make Christianity and biblical teachings relevant to the African context. Unless we know what it is that we need to renew and transform, we cannot make progress in the transformation. Until we know and understand the people we wish to transform, we will find it difficult to speak to them.

In this chapter I will focus on the theological, psychological, philosophical, moral and ethical principles of African Traditional Religion in order to understand how these influence our understanding of evil and our response to sin.[3]

Fundamental Theological Beliefs

The details of African Traditional Religion vary from region to region, but all variants share five fundamentals beliefs: belief in impersonal powers, belief in spirit beings, belief in divinities or gods, belief in a Supreme Being, and belief in a hierarchy of spiritual beings and powers.

Belief in impersonal powers

In African thought, the whole of creation is pregnant with spiritual powers that lie behind what is material, physical and visible. Some objects are assumed to be endowed with more power than others, and the potency, efficacy and durability of the power varies from object to object and from place to place. These impersonal powers are contagious and can be transferred by contact with powerful objects or by purely spiritual means. They can also be directed to specific destinations to accomplish good or evil.

Certain people are believed to be able to accomplish good by harnessing the impersonal powers associated with natural objects, plants and animals to produce medicine, magic, charms and amulets. But wicked human beings and wicked spirit beings can use these same powers for evil. Traditional Africans feel that they are at the mercy of the benevolence or malevolence of those who can control these powers. Thus life is dangerous and full of uncertainties.

Africans are tempted to see sin as another form of impersonal spiritual power. But Scripture teaches that sin is not simply the product of outside influence but comes from within human nature. Nor is it simply an irresistible contagion; we have a choice about whether to sin. What is external to us is evil, and so are the temptations that come our way. But it is only when evil is appropriated or taken in that it gives birth to sin. Thus James can say,

When tempted, no one should say, "God is tempting me". For God cannot be tempted by evil, nor does he tempt anyone; but each person is tempted when they are dragged away by their own evil desire and enticed. Then, after desire has conceived, it gives birth to sin; and sin, when it is full-grown, gives birth to death. (Jas 1:13–15)

African Christians who want to cling to their traditional beliefs regarding the power of witchcraft and sorcery point out that the Bible also refers to the exercise of supernatural powers. So it does. But Christianity and African Traditional Religion have very different understandings of the source and content of this power.

Belief in spirit beings

For traditional Africans, the world is not only filled with supernatural powers but is also inhabited by spirit beings. There is a close relationship between the spirit beings and the impersonal powers, but they are distinct. The beings are believed to inhabit certain trees, rocks, mountains, caves, rivers, lakes, forests, burial grounds, animals, human beings, the skies, the ground and other sites, carved or moulded objects, charms, amulets – the list is endless.

The spirits are ranked hierarchically in accordance with their power and role in the spirit world. First comes the Creator, followed by lesser deities, object-embodied spirits, ancestral spirits and miscellaneous non-human spirits. Human beings stand between this host of spirits and the world of nature.

Spirit beings can be categorized as either human or non-human. Human spirits are the living dead, that is, the spirits of the ancestors who are close to human beings and serve as their guardians. Non-human spirits may be either good or evil, depending on whether they use the powers with which they are endowed to bring blessings or curses. In a sense, the supernatural realm is a battleground in which spirit beings use their powers to influence the course of human life.

Spirit beings can be malicious and capricious, and so it is important to be wise and tactful in one's dealings with them and to avoid angering, provoking or injuring them. Those who stay on good terms with the spirits are happier. Consequently, those who wish to be successful, or merely to enjoy well-being, consult specialists who have experience of and access to mystical and spiritual powers. These specialists include medicine men, rainmakers, mediums, diviners, sorcerers, magicians, witches and all others who have the ability to manipulate spirit beings.

It is also believed that spirit beings can take possession of someone, and can only be expelled by exorcism.[4] This belief leads many African Christians to assume that sinful behaviour is caused by demonic spirits taking possession of a human being. Thus there is talk about a spirit of anger, a spirit of adultery, a spirit of jealousy, a spirit of stealing, and so on. Whereas Westerners interpret such words as figures of speech, African believers often mean them to be taken literally. Consequently, their way of dealing with sin is to attempt to cast out the spirit of the specific sin. However, the Bible never calls for exorcism as a way of dealing with sin. What the Bible calls for is repentance, confession and forgiveness.

Scripture and African Traditional Religion are in agreement that supernatural powers can influence a human being or an environment. Spiritual powers do exist and can indeed exert power over people, territories or places. But the way they do this is through sinful acts, which provide them with an opportunity to establish a foothold in our lives. As we continue to sin, this foothold can grow to a stronghold that dominates our life. The only way we can be freed from this domination is by confessing the very particular sins that have allowed the building of these strongholds. God holds us accountable for our sins. We cannot put the blame on demons, other people, heredity or society. These are only forces around us that reinforce our own sinfulness.

Belief in many divinities

Scholars argue about whether the many divinities of African Traditional Religion are worshipped as gods or whether they are only intermediaries, through whom Africans worship the one God. Those who hold to the latter view argue that traditional sacrifices, offerings and prayers are not ultimately directed to the divinities or the ancestors themselves but are directed to God. This argument seeks to remove the stigma of idolatry from African Traditional Religion. But it fails the biblical test. The Bible defines idolatry as the worship of anything other than the triune God.

Divinities are associated with various aspects of life. There are, for example, divinities of the sea or the waters, rain, thunder, fertility, health and sickness, planting and harvest, as well as tribal, clan or family deities. African divinities take the forms of mountains, rivers, forests, mother earth, the sun, the moon, the stars and ancestors. This plurality of divinities, even within one ethnic group or community, clearly indicates that traditional religious thought is open to religious pluralism.

Monotheistic religions like Christianity and Islam may have introduced what is called henotheism to the African world view, that is, the worship of one god without denying the existence of other gods. Traditional beliefs can accommodate the worship of the Christian God along with other gods without creating any serious theological crisis for the believer. A plurality of gods or divinities permits a plurality of beliefs, practices and behaviours in one religion. There is plenty of scope for assimilation, adaptation and domestication of new gods or divinities into the old religion.

This situation has a profound influence on the theology of many African Christians, who can hold two opposing views without experiencing any conflict. Thus many worship Jesus Christ while still clinging to their ancestral beliefs and worship. This weakens their understanding of sin and of the effective solution to it.

Belief in a Supreme Being

Some of the pioneering anthropologists and missionaries denied that Africans had any awareness or perception of God. They were wrong. It is now firmly established that Africans do have a concept of a universal God and Creator.[5] It is, however, also generally agreed that traditional Africans do not actively worship this Supreme Being, who is perceived as remote and not involved in this world. He may sometimes be mentioned in prayers, songs and some religious ceremonies, but sacrifices, offerings and prayers are made to lesser divinities and the ancestors.

This attitude to the Supreme Being weakens the development of a strong Christian spirituality and an intimate relationship with God. This, in turn, leads to a lack of a strong concept of holiness and righteousness and an absence of commitment to godly living.

Belief in a hierarchy of spiritual beings

One component of the apparent disregard for the Supreme Being in traditional Africa is the fundamental belief that all spiritual beings and powers form part of a hierarchical order with different spheres of authority, power and influence. The Supreme Being enjoys the highest position. Other divinities occupy lower positions, and below them come various spirit beings. This hierarchy is fluid, and the distinction between spirits may be vague and their powers diffused.

Traditional Africans are familiar with the place of various spirits in the spiritual hierarchy, their power and influence, territoriality, legitimacy and role. They seek help from the spirit presumed to have the greatest power in relation to their particular situation. Thus even African Christians do not necessarily seek help from God or Jesus (who seem to them to be out of touch with reality). Instead, they prefer to deal with beings whose power is directly felt in this world. Acutely aware of the work of evil and of the wicked forces that afflict people, they turn to witchdoctors, mediums and wizards for help. Mediums are perceived as more powerful than pastors when it comes to dealing with demons.

When African Christians fear witchcraft and worship the spirits of dead ancestors, they are acting on the basis of their experience and the reality of life that surrounds them. Unless the power of the cross of Christ is seen and felt to be superior to that of the spirits and ancestors, they cannot be liberated from these traditional ways.

Fundamental Psychological Beliefs

Living in a world that is full of unseen, unpredictable powers controlled by malicious and capricious spirits inevitably has profound psychological consequences. Five particular attitudes dominate the psychology of those raised within the orbit of the traditional African world view:

- Fear of spiritual powers and of the unpredictable contingencies of life, before which humans are powerless.
- Lack of consolation, peace and comfort. Traditional religious rites, rituals, ceremonies, sacrifices and offerings provide only temporary comfort. Indeed, they often enhance fear, rather than reducing it, especially when they have to be repeated time after time.
- Little differentiation between good and evil. The numerous spirits and gods often exhibit contradictory characteristics, being both good

and evil. It is thus difficult to make any clear distinction between good and evil, for both good and evil can co-inhabit a god, a spirit or a human being.

- Belief that one's fate had already been determined by superior powers and that it cannot be changed. This fatalism breeds hopelessness and resignation.
- Pursuit of spiritual power. Africans are pragmatic. While they believe in fate, they also believe that those with sufficient access to spiritual power can change their circumstances or avert evil. Thus they search for the life force that will enable them to control and manipulate powers, rather than being manipulated by them. Magesa claims that pursuit of this force is the only dominant "ideology" or reason for living for an African, and that the search for it provides the basis for African life, morality and ethics.[6] To obtain this force, humans need to enter into alliances with spirit beings and supernatural powers, which themselves need human beings in order to survive. The way to communicate with them, manipulate them and control them is through rituals, ceremonies, sacrifices and offerings.

When Africans become Christians, their psychology does not change overnight, but continues to influence their understanding of Christian teachings. Sin, spirituality and power are understood in terms of rituals, ceremonies, religious exuberance and ecstasy. But effectively dealing with sin involves more than just rituals and ceremonies. It involves the cross of Christ, and all that it stands for in terms of redemption, sanctification, deliverance, repentance and forgiveness of sin.

Fundamental Philosophical Beliefs

There is always a profound interaction between a society's philosophy, that is, its understanding of the world, and its theology and behaviour. Thus, it is important to understand the philosophical foundations that underlie the traditional world view. In his study of animism, Philip Steyne identified the four basic philosophical foundations of a traditional African world view as holism, spiritualism, dynamism and communalism.[7] To these, I have added a fifth, fatalism. The combination of the theological and psychological beliefs discussed in the previous sections and the philosophical beliefs presented here creates a world view that dominates traditional African thought and determines its moral laws.

Holism

Western thinking tends to be dualistic, but traditional Africans have an organic or holistic view of life that sees all things as existing in a state of complex interdependency. They do not draw a clear boundary between the physical and spiritual dimensions of life. There is no sharp distinction between secular and religious activities, between one's work and one's community responsibilities. Thus African Traditional Religion does not have a creed. Beliefs do not have to be learned; they are caught, passed on and lived.

Steyne defines holism in the following terms:

> The world interacts with itself. The sky, the spirits, the earth, the physical world, the living, and the deceased all act, interact, and react in consort. One works on the other and one part can't exist nor be explained without the other. The universe, the spirit world and man are all part of the same fabric. Each needs the other to activate it."[8]

Because nature, humanity and the spirit world constitute one fluid coherent unit, there are clearly pantheistic elements in African holism. In fact, nature is defined as comprising all that is visible as well as impersonal powers and spirit beings. There is no discord between the spirit world and the world of nature; both combine harmoniously and happenings in the spiritual world have visible effects in the natural world.

The concept of harmony means that the physical activities of humans and spirits affect the balance or harmony in the cosmos. This aspect of African thought is in accord with what is revealed in the Bible. Adam and Eve's fall in Eden led to the ground, or the earth, being cursed by God. The physical world was affected by human sin. Sin, a spiritual phenomenon, has devastating physical consequences. Traditional religion has a clearer understanding of this than most Christians.

Africans do not live in a confused world of non-integrated parts. Life is mysterious, but it is part of a whole. And that whole is governed by a law of harmony, the goal of which is to maintain a state of agreement or peacefulness. The traditional African seeks to balance life so as to enjoy a harmonious and peaceful existence with the entire world and especially with the spirit world.

Those thought to be wayward were asked to look within to find out where they had broken harmony or relationships, and were then told to offer gifts and sacrifices to restore peace and find forgiveness. Similarly, Christians who are experiencing misfortune are thought to have broken harmony with the spirits of their ancestors and may be asked to offer blood sacrifices or perform certain other rituals to appease them. In this traditional world view, sin is viewed as a lack of harmony or a broken relationship with the ancestors, spirits and the natural world. Atonement is the way to restore harmony and relationships.

But rituals can be used not only to restore harmony but also to gain life force, and Africans who become Christians still cherish belief in this power, rather than replacing it with a belief in Christ-power.

Spiritualism

In the previous section I stated that traditional beliefs do not distinguish between the material and the spiritual worlds. It might be truer to say that this world in essence is spiritual rather than material, and that life is saturated with supernatural possibilities. Steyne puts it this way:

> The whole universe is interconnected through the will and the power contained in both animate and inanimate objects. Everything man is, does, handles, projects, and interacts with is interpenetrated with the spiritual. His socio-cultural structures, down to their finest details, are under the control of the spiritual powers or forces. Nothing in man's environment escapes the influence or the manipulation of the spirit world. The world is more spiritual than it is physical and it is spiritually upheld.[9]

In Africa, answers to questions about the meaning of life ('Why' questions) are almost always couched in spiritual terms. When trouble comes in the form of disease, natural disasters or untimely death, traditional Africans look beyond the obvious physical causes and consult religious specialists to find the ultimate spiritual cause. In old Africa, Africans would consult the oracles to obtain divine answers about what they should do. The Jews of the Old Testament did the same, and Christians still seek the will of God through prayer and fasting.

The philosophy of spiritualism both draws on and supports pantheistic polytheistic theology and is reflected in the moral laws and religious practices that govern the interrelationship and integration of spirit beings and humans.

Christian Westerners sometimes misinterpret African spirituality as evidence of a deep understanding of how the Holy Spirit works in human life. But often the focus is less on the Holy Spirit than on cosmic spirits. Yet this rich spiritual foundation has enormous potential for good. Failure to recognize the similarity between this traditional spiritual world view and the biblical world view has deprived the church in Africa of authentic biblical and Christian theology for Africans.

Dynamism

Dynamism asserts the importance of both spirits and power. The combination of these two produces spirit power or supernatural power, which is of the utmost importance in traditional philosophy:

> Life's essential quest is to secure power and use it. Not to have power or access to it produces great anxiety in the face of spirit caprice and the rigors of life. A life without power is not worth living ... Power offers man control of his uncertain world. The search for and acquisition of power supersedes any commitment to ethics or morality. Whatever is empowering is right.[10]

Power can be obtained in a variety of ways, including:

> ritual manipulation ... in the form of sacrifices, offerings, taboos, charms, fetishes, ceremonies, even witchcraft and sorcery ... The power may also be secured by the laying on of hands or by encountering a spirit being, either directly or through ritual means. The power may be transmitted through contact with persons of superior religious status or by using clothing or something previously associated with such a person. How it is secured is a secondary concern. It must be acquired whatever the cost.[11]

The all-consuming search for power exerts an enormous influence on morality and ethics and on the relationship between humans and spirit beings and forces. It also affects how traditional Africans assess the potency or efficacy of a new religion or ritual. A powerless religion is perceived as valueless. A powerless Christianity can have hardly any impact in a society so pregnant with dynamism or spirit power.

Traditional religion is very clear in its understanding and use of spirit power. So is the Bible. But the biblical theology of power has yet to be fully developed by African Christians to address the traditional pursuit of power. The lack of good and relevant Christian theology of Christ-power has driven many Christians to search for traditional spirit power.

Communalism

If everything that exists is in an organic relation to everything else that exists, as discussed in the earlier section on holism, then the same applies to how human beings interact. People are not individuals, living in a state of independence, but are part of a community, living in relationships and interdependence. One does not claim personal rights and freedoms; rather, one fulfils one's communal obligations and duties. Van der Walt lists some forty characteristics of African communalism that contrast with Western individualism.[12] These characteristics can be summarized in terms of communal self-respect, interdependence, survival of the community, group assurance, cooperation and harmony, affiliation and shared duties.

This concept of community is not restricted to the community of human beings alone, but embraces a communal attitude to the world of the spirits and ancestors as well as to the world of nature.

- *Communalism in relation to fellow humans.* A traditional African community consisted of clans with different histories, emblems and taboos and also their sub-clans and kindred. This kinship-based organization is very important in understanding the community, its religious beliefs, behaviour, practices, morality, ethics and ethnicity. The most powerful principle of social organization is the concept of brotherhood, and all members have affinity, loyalty and obligations to the blood-community. This system of relationships has been seriously disrupted by the introduction of universal religions such as Christianity,

Islam, and modernism. It has also been affected by the re-alignment of tribal units in the new modern states. The changes have resulted in many social and political problems, including fears, suspicions, rivalry, tensions, and conflicts among the various ethnic and tribal groups.

- *Communalism in relation to ancestors and the spirit world.* The human community is not only intimately related to its living members but also to the spirit world – the community of the ancestors who now live in the past – and to those still to be born. The life of the community of the living is controlled, maintained, and protected by the community of the ancestors. Communal life in this kinship system can be described as ancestrally chartered. Steyne observes that outside of this ancestral kinship "there lies no possibility of life" and that "personhood is meaningless" apart from these ancestral kinships and relationships.[13] The communal perspective also has important implications in regard to the spirit world that permeates everyday existence. If humans are part of a holistic community with the spirit world, it is as important to avoid offending the spirits as it is to avoid offending one's human community.

- *Communalism in relation to nature.* The law of holism stresses that everything is part of an organic whole. Thus people seek to understand the mysterious forces that lie behind natural phenomena. Any natural object may carry a message that needs to be deciphered. Some animals or plants may be totems, with specific kinship affinity or religious or medicinal uses. The potency, value and efficacy of a totem is determined by its nature, and can be enhanced or reduced by other objects in its proximity. Animals and birds for sacrifices, objects for offerings, and ritual or ceremonial sites or groves are carefully selected on the basis of their religious value and efficacy. Nature provides a vast array of contact points with the world of the spirit.

Traditional Africans are so caught up in dealing with all these relationships that their dealings with God take a secondary position. Sin is viewed not so much as offending God but as offending against kinship and communal values, the spirit world and the natural world. It is seen as communal rather than personal. Western missionaries, however, influenced by Western individualism, tended to emphasize personal sin. The result has been that African Christians tend to focus only on personal dealings with sin and neglect communal and social means of dealing with it. They miss the truth that the church of Jesus Christ as a new community and new humanity has profound communal values.

Kinship values rooted in blood relationships are positive in that they develop very strong affinity, obligations and loyalties within the kinship community. However, they also have a negative aspect in that they feed into tribalism, ethnicity and racism, leading to communal and social sins as regards the treatment of strangers and outsiders, and spiritual idolatry as regards maintaining loyalty to the ancestors, spirits and traditional divinities.

Fatalism

The concepts of destiny and fate in the traditional world view are closely related to the belief in spirits and mysterious powers. Destiny is the belief that the position, place and status of individuals or groups have been predetermined by some external, supernatural force. Fate is similar to destiny in that it means that certain events are predetermined to happen. The end result of a strong belief in destiny and fate is fatalism, "a doctrine that events are fixed in advance for all time in such a manner that human beings are powerless to change them".[14] One's destiny cannot be changed, and should be accepted with gratitude. Any attempt to change it will have devastating consequences.

However, one can be hindered from fulfilling one's destiny by others or by spiritual powers. Spirits and mysterious powers control the world of fate, and God does not seem to be active in protecting man against their evil activities. One has to find one's own protection and security.

The apparent lack of active protection from God has great theological implications for traditional Africans, especially in their search for spiritual power that will offer them protection and security.

Fundamental Moral and Ethical Beliefs

Our world view influences our attitudes, behaviour and social practice and thus also our moral and ethical beliefs. This is also true in Africa, where the fundamental philosophical principles underlying the traditional world view are the basis of what are known as the traditional moral laws. Holism finds expression in the law of harmony; spiritualism finds expression in the law of the spirit; dynamism finds expression in the law of power; communalism finds expression in the law of kinship; and fatalism finds expression in the law of destiny.

These laws should not be thought of in isolation from each other. All are interdependent. An action that may seem inexplicable in terms of one moral law may make sense when all the moral laws are considered together.

Law of harmony

The law of harmony is derived from the holistic world view that holds in harmony, or balance, the spirit world, the natural world and the human world. These worlds are interdependent and complementary, and the greatest duty of human beings is to learn the art of living in harmony with them all.

Any distortion of or damage to the cosmic harmony results in suffering. Thus the pursuit of harmony takes precedence over everything else. What is "right" or "just" is regarded as far less important than whatever holds things in balance or brings the desired results. Thus answers to ethical questions do not focus on the morality of the actions but on their goal. Any means can be justified by the pursuit of harmony and peace.

Christianity, by contrast, pays far more attention to motives than to actions. Even righteous behaviour can be condemned if it is done with the wrong motives.

The traditional understanding of the law of harmony tends to weaken the biblical teaching that God is the only true source of peace and harmony. At the fall, our harmony with God and nature was broken by sin, but Christ's death reconciles us to God, to each other, to nature, and to ourselves. The law of harmony should now find positive expression in the new humanity within the church, the body of Christ, within which communitarian values and ethics based on the gospel of Christ can be used to maintain harmony and broker reconciliation and forgiveness among Christians.

Law of the spirit

The law of the spirit reflects the traditional African understanding that the world is in essence spiritual and full of mystical powers and forces. Reality does not consist in what is apparent, but in what lies behind and guides life's phenomena. Things are not to be accepted at face value because events and actions are controlled by unseen spiritual forces. The question to ask is neither "why" nor "how", but "who or what is behind what is happening?"

The answer to this question is what gives spiritual meaning in life. But this meaning is rooted in expediency and pragmatism rather than morality. Spiritual meaning must be sought, regardless of its source. Thus rather than being a sign of true spirituality, a preoccupation with spiritual matters may simply reflect someone's focus on a specific spiritual goal or search for spiritual powers.

Traditional religion recognizes God as the Eternal Spirit and thus the ultimate reality. But it is content to owe allegiance to spirit beings or powers that are subordinate to the Eternal Spirit. The answers these beings provide take precedence over moral obedience to the will of the Creator.

By contrast, the moral goal in Christianity is not to find out what is happening to us or why, but to do the will of God. The true meaning and purpose of life is rooted only in God who is Eternal Spirit, and not in some lesser spirit beings or subordinate spirit powers. For Christians, God is the only legitimate source of true spiritual meaning, purpose and power.

Law of power

The pursuit of spiritual meaning rapidly shades into the pursuit of spirit power. Traditional Africans believe very strongly that their destiny and well-being are controlled and manipulated by unseen mysterious powers. Thus they look for power that can enable them to predict, control and manipulate spirit powers and forces for their own benefit.

Traditional Africans can access spirit power by consulting specialists who have access to these powers through rituals, divination, ceremonies, sacrifices, incantations, symbolism, witchcraft, sorcery, charms, fetishes, and white and black magic. The potency of each means, each spirit being, and each mysterious power depends very much upon its position in the hierarchy of powers and spiritual beings in the spirit world. Some are more powerful or influential than others. For this reason, the search for more potent and powerful spiritual agents and powers is a strong driving force in traditional Africa. It leads some Christians to dabble in things that God has forbidden, such as witchcraft, sorcery and divination.

In Christianity, God is the only source of legitimate power and he holds and sustains his creation under his providential and sustaining power. Any spirit power obtained from other sources is illegitimate and open to condemnation. However, in traditional Africa, the pursuit of spiritual and mystical powers tends to take precedence over moral obedience to the will of God.

Law of kinship

The law of kinship derives from communalism, the belief that protection, meaning, identity and status are rooted in the kinship community or blood-group. The community is governed by the kinship values of loyalty, affinity and obligations. One result is that kinship interests, group interests, territorial interests, tribal interests or racial interests take precedence over all other social and ethical considerations.

Those who are not part of the kinship community or the blood-group are all strangers or outsiders and cannot expect to be treated in accordance with the same moral and ethical principles that prevail within the kinship community. The result is an ethical relativism that has no universal standards. Tribalism and racism are prevalent.

Colonialism and missionary Christianity challenged African traditional kinship and communitarian values but failed to transform them. Consequently Africa is rife with all manner of crises, including genocide and civil wars. Many atrocities are committed.

The challenge we face as Christians is how to transform the traditional kinship values and apply them in an all-inclusive new community, the body of Christ.

Summary

African Christians who have a shallow knowledge of the teachings of the Bible and Christian theology will have an understanding of evil and sin that is rooted in their traditional religious beliefs and world view. Their pervasive spirituality will be infused with spirit power whose source is not the Eternal Spirit of God. Such spirituality inevitably leads to spiritual idolatry, that is, the worship of surrogate spirit beings and spirit powers.

God, the real Eternal Spirit, is often perceived only as the last port of call, to be remembered only when all else has failed. God is almost absent in the day-to-day affairs of life. It is thus vitally important that we look at who God really is, and at his relationship to sin.

3
GOD AND SIN

As a young boy, I often wondered why sin ever appeared on earth. If I were God, I would never have allowed it. I would have brought Satan to book immediately and sent him straight to hell. After all, if Satan had not been there, Adam and Eve would not have fallen and I would not still be struggling with sin.

Others too have blamed God for the problem of sin, saying that he should have created Adam and Eve in such a way that it would have been impossible for them to sin. Others ask how the all-powerful and all-knowing God could have allowed sin or evil to exist at all. They end up questioning the supreme power of God and the Christian answer in the gospel of Christ.

This type of view is even stronger among those who come from a traditional religious background and believe that sinful or evil acts are caused by forces beyond our control. If God, the Eternal Spirit, permits these forces to work, then surely he is to blame when we fall into sin?

To be able to respond to this question, we need to do more thinking about what God is like. We need to move beyond the type of image I had of God when I was a young boy. I pictured him as an old man with a very big eye and a very long beard, holding a very long smoking pipe. This was how I and my friends visualized a typical African elder, and we thought of God as the supreme elder. What other option did we have?

Many renowned philosophers have made this same mistake. They believe that what we call "God" is only a mental projection of what is truly human. When humans place this projection above the skies, they call him a High God.

This image of God was not the only misleading idea I picked up in childhood. I also learned that God is not always trustworthy. Whenever calamity struck and a young man died, his mourning mother would complain bitterly that God had not been merciful, kind or protective. The women would sing songs accusing God, spirit beings, and even other people of treacherously causing his death.

These women were making the same mistake that many others have done at times of tragedy. They were defining God as wicked, or unkind, or uncaring, or unloving on the basis of their circumstances. How could someone like Job explain his suffering as not coming from the hand of God when he knew that he was innocent of any wrongdoing? The only way Job's friends could defend God's character was by attacking Job. In their crude theology, only the wicked suffer, never the righteous. Therefore Job must be guilty of concealing some great sin. But they, too, had a mistaken view of God and evil.

So where can we turn for an accurate understanding of the nature of God? The best place to look is in Scripture. There we can see the attributes of God and begin to understand why we can rule out any association of sin or evil with God.

God's Nature

If you compare the attributes of God in the prayers, songs, ritual incantations and oral history of African Traditional Religion and his attributes in the Bible, you will find that many of them are similar. This is not surprising, for in both human nature and general nature, God is revealed in much the same way in all human societies. There is even an extent to which Africans who have a thorough knowledge of African traditional beliefs about God stand a better chance of understanding biblical teachings on God than those who know nothing about them. Our African perceptions of God can help clarify and strengthen our biblical understanding of God.

However, because of human sinfulness, our perception of God is always clouded. That is why we need the special revelation of Scripture and Jesus Christ to renew and transform our traditional thinking about God, just as Christianity transformed Jewish thinking, as explained in the book of Hebrews.

God is a Trinity

For many years, I struggled with the concept of the Trinity. To avoid having to try to explain it, I settled for it being a mystery. It was easy to accept it as such, for there are many things in traditional Africa that are best left as mysteries. However, although the nature of the Trinity is mysterious, the Bible does tell us some things about it. It clearly reveals that God is one (Deut 6:4 – "Hear O Israel: The Lord our God, the Lord is one") and that he revealed himself in the New Testament in three persons: God the Father, God the Son and God the Holy Spirit.

God the Father is introduced in the Old Testament as the creator of heaven and earth. He did this through the word of his power, thus revealing himself through his word and power. He is the same God who was honoured as the Creator by our African ancestors. However, in the Bible he is also revealed as the God of Abraham, Isaac and Jacob and as the Father of our Lord Jesus Christ.

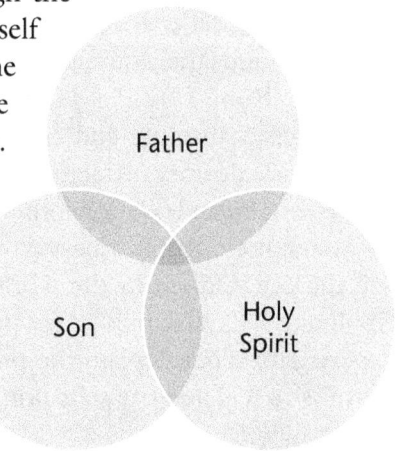

Holy Trinity (Matt 28:19)

Jesus Christ is introduced in the New Testament as the final revelation of God. In the Old Testament, he was revealed as the Word of God. At the incarnation, this Word of God became the Son of God. He is co-eternal with God the Father (John 1:1–14; Col 1:15; Heb 1:1–3). Some African Christians tend to interpret Christ's role through the lens of African Traditional Religion. They acknowledge God as the Supreme Being, and see Jesus as a lesser being, although occupying a very high position. However, it is not enough to describe Jesus as just an Ancestor, an Elder, and a Healer. These titles reflect his role but not his position as God the Son who is fully and equally God.

The Holy Spirit is introduced in the Old Testament as the Spirit or Power of God and in the New Testament as the Holy Spirit, the Comforter. In the Old Testament, he only came upon people to help them to accomplish some specific tasks, and would leave once those tasks had been accomplished. But in the New Testament and at Pentecost, he came not only upon people, but also to indwell or fill them. He is not an influence, force, or one of the spirits, as some would think in Africa, but a Person in the Trinity.

Without the final revelation of God in Christ, the problem of sin and evil has no solution. The cross of Jesus Christ is the only means by which God deals with sin in humans and evil in the world. He is the only way of salvation (John 14:6; Acts 4:12).

God is sovereign

To say that God is sovereign means that he is "the ultimate, personal authority and the source of all authority (Dan 4:34–35; cf. 2:21; 7:13–14; Rom 13:1)."[15] He is the sole owner of the entire universe. He exercises absolute and supreme power over his creation and is the Creator, Redeemer, Ruler, Lawgiver, Judge and Lord of the entire universe. African traditional theology agrees with these general terms.

Sometimes people question whether God is sovereign when they see the evil and sin in the world. They argue that God's power must be limited. Traditional Africans, however, do not question God's sovereignty. They explain the presence of evil and sin in light of God's permissive will and the rebellion of lesser spirit beings.

God is eternal

Our minds cannot handle the idea of eternity. The very idea of God having no beginning or end is unimaginable. This is yet another way in which God is bigger than our minds and intelligence. We can only affirm the mystery that has been revealed to us in the Bible: "From everlasting to everlasting you are God" (Ps 90:2).

The Bible teaches that God is eternal, self-existing and self-sufficient. He is eternally a living being who is uncreated. Both his eternal existence and his eternal being come only from himself and from nothing else.

There is no debate about this truth in Africa. The God of our ancestors never dies, just as the God of Abraham, Isaac and Jacob never dies.

God is the eternal Word

The Bible says: "In the beginning was the Word and Word was with God and the Word was God" (John 1:1). This is an amazing and puzzling statement. How can God be his Word and his Word also be God? We can never resolve all of this mystery, but what we do know is that Jesus is the Word of God, and the Word of God is Jesus. He is the true revelation of God in human flesh (John 1:1–14). Jesus is not just a lesser spirit being who aided God in creation. Nor is he a spirit being who has amassed enough power to became a force that must be reckoned with. Nor is he a reincarnated ancestor. No, he is the incarnation of God, the true God in human form.

The spoken word is very powerful in traditional Africa. People tremble at the words of elders and ancestors that bring blessings or curses. Incantations, too, demonstrate the power of words to accomplish things. But Christ, the Eternal Word of God, is stronger than all such things.

God is eternal spirit

The Bible states that "God is spirit" (John 4:24), but if so he cannot be seen. How then can we know him? How do we differentiate him from the other spirit beings that throng the world of traditional Africa? How is his power different from the supernatural power that Africans seek?

The answer is that God revealed his special spiritual power in Jesus Christ, who is the Word of God and the Son of God, and also in the Holy Spirit, who is the Power of God and the Spirit of God. The cross of Christ and the resurrection of Jesus Christ introduced Christ-power, which is above all other powers. He has made all his enemies his footstool and he sits at the right hand of the Father (Heb 1:13).

Africans need to know that the power of Christ and of the Holy Spirit are eternal and sovereign over all the temporal spirit powers that they are pursuing in order to accumulate life force. They also need to know that as Spirit, God is immutable, that is, unchanging, always constant. He is the same yesterday, today and for ever (Mal 3:6; James 1:17; Heb 13:8). Moreover, because he is Spirit, God is all-knowing (omniscient), present everywhere (omnipresent) and all-powerful (omnipotent).

God is good

The presence of sin, evil and suffering in the universe is a problem that confronts all religions. African Traditional Religion explains their presence in terms of witchcraft, which is evil personified. All sickness, death and natural evil or calamities are caused by spirit beings and spirit power, whose malevolence is to be feared. Although all these spirits are subordinate to the Eternal Spirit, he allows them free rein in this world.

By contrast, the Bible teaches that creation is good and that God is good. He is morally perfect, and all that he does is rooted in his character. His eternal goodness is the absolute opposite of sin and evil. God cannot think evil. He cannot sin. We have no grounds whatever for associating him with evil. This Christian teaching breathes hope, rather than fear.

Our hope is even stronger because of the revelation of a superpower, Christ-power, that has defeated all subordinate spirits. Through the cross, Christ reconciled God and humanity, God and nature, and ourselves, nature and others. Evil and its by-product, sin, have been defeated by Christ. The book of Revelation shows that God will bring an end to all works of evil, whether physical or spiritual. He will replace the old heaven and earth with a new one. God, who is eternal goodness, is not the problem but rather the only solution to evil and sin.

God is wise

Africans associate wisdom with age and have deep respect for older people. The former ages are thought to have been wiser than the latter ones. Wisdom is rooted in our origins, not in the present. The "now" has no wisdom. The young are dangerous and unreliable, but older people can be trusted.

Given that we associate wisdom with older people, how much more should we attribute it to the eternal God (Ps 136:5; Prov 3:19)? The goodness of God reveals his wisdom as he evaluates what he has done and sees that all he has created is good. As a good and wise Creator, he has built purpose and meaning into his creation. This gives his creation a moral character. But God's ways are different from human ways. The Bible talks of God's way of salvation as wisdom, but to us it seems that the cross is foolishness. God uses the weak things of life to bring shame upon the strong (1 Cor 1:18–31).

Africans cherish wisdom. They love it more than food. It is the highest philosophical virtue and value. How encouraging is it then that he who gets God, gets wisdom (Prov 9:10) and that Christ is the wisdom and power of God (1 Cor 1:18–31).

God is holy

Sometimes it is very difficult to state clearly what holiness really means when applied to God. We are quick to identify God's holiness with purity and the absence of sin. But his holiness goes much further than that.

> Holy is the way God is. To be holy He does not conform to a standard. He is that standard. He is absolutely holy with an infinite, incomprehensible fullness of purity that is incapable of being other than it is. Because He is holy, all His attributes are holy; that is, whatever we think of as belonging to God must be thought of as holy ... God is holy and He has made holiness the moral condition necessary to the health of His universe ... The holiness of God, the wrath of God, and the health of the creation are inseparably united."[16]

Like Judaism in the Old Testament, African Traditional Religion emphasizes the need to distinguish between what is clean and unclean, as well as purification, ceremonial washings and abstinence. For example, men who are going to war or going hunting must not lie with their wives or any woman. Ceremonial bathing and washing are prerequisites for obtaining a certain life force. These are human rules that pertain to clean and unclean social practices, but God's holiness is greater than these. His very nature is holy. He does not have to make himself holy by washing or cleansing.

As human beings we are innately and inherently sinful; no amount of ceremonial washing can make us clean. But as the book of Hebrews reminds us, the blood of Christ cleanses us from sin (Heb 9:11–10:18). All the blood sacrifices of African Traditional Religion that were designed to bring cleansing and to provide spirit power or life force have been supplanted by the death of Jesus Christ on the cross.

God is righteous

We have just read that God is good and that all that he does is good. So no wonder we are surprised to find that the Bible includes statements such as "God repented" or "regretted" doing something, or "changed his mind" (Gen 6:6; 1 Chr 21:15). And what do we make of the fact that God commanded the Israelites to wipe out the Canaanites? Do we have grounds to question God's sovereignty, holiness, goodness and righteousness?

No, because what we are failing to understand is that both creatures and creation have fallen and are no longer in their original state. Neither the moral nor the physical order now function perfectly and harmoniously. As a result, both moral and natural evil feature prominently in the universe, where God uses them to accomplish his purpose and will.

Africans who wish to be righteous follow the traditions of the elders and ancestors and observe all kinds of rituals, ceremonies, feast days and taboos. But if they make any mistake in a ritual, it is ineffective, and any accidental failure to maintain a taboo is punished. It is thus a relief to discover that God has revealed another path to righteousness in the gospel of Christ, "a righteousness that is by faith from first to last" (Rom 1:17). God's righteousness is not obtained by knowing formulas or observing laws but by faith in Jesus Christ. It is his gift to us based upon the cross of Christ and not our performance of any ritual.

God is just

God is both righteous and just. These two qualities are very closely linked. "Righteousness can be defined as moral equity. Justice is the illustration of this moral equity. In righteousness God reveals his love for holiness. In justice God reveals his hatred for sin."[17] Here is another definition of God's justice:

> Justice is the outgoing of God's holiness with reference to moral (or immoral) creatures ... Since the creature is unholy and unjust, it follows that God in his justice must vindicate His holy character and maintain His creation as an expression of that holy character. A holy God if He maintains a creation, must maintain a holy creation, and must be hostile to all things in it, which are in violation of His own holiness.[18]

Because God is just and utterly opposed to sin, he expects us to have the same attitude. Sadly the African kinship values that are rooted in blood relationships deny many in modern Africa justice, equality and freedom. Ethics and morality are seen as limited by kinship boundaries. The application of God's universal requirement of justice is limited to my kinship community or tribe or race. The universal God of justice is domesticated as a tribal god and is stripped of his universality. This God does not cross kinship, tribal or racial boundaries.

But God in his revelation in Jesus Christ changes that. He does not destroy the kinship values of affinity, loyalty, and obligations, but he renews and transforms them by creating a new humanity, an all-inclusive messianic community of believers. The kinship boundary is widened to include all others, and is not limited only to those who are like us.

God is angry

How can a holy God be angry? Wouldn't anger destroy his holiness and righteousness? These questions show that we do not understand the true nature of God, for his anger is rooted in his holiness, righteousness and justice. African Traditional Religion understands this point much better than the average Christian. The type of anger we are talking about here is the same type of anger that bereaved mothers show when they are angry with God for allowing their children to die (although these mothers are wrong to see God as uncaring and as the source of evil).

God's anger is without any fault. It is the result of his revulsion against sin. Thus it can be called a holy anger, that is, an anger that is not motivated by or rooted in sin.

God is true

Jesus speaks of his father as "the only true God" (John 17:3), using a word that means "established, certain, or faithful."[19] He also speaks of himself as personifying truth, saying: "I am the way, and the truth, and the life. No one comes to the Father except through me" (John 14:6). Truthfulness characterizes God's very nature. It is "that attribute of the divine nature in virtue of which God's being and God's knowledge eternally conform to each other."[20] In other words, God does not lie (Titus 1:2). He sets the ultimate standard of truth.

Because God is true, so is his word. It is reliable, dependable and trustworthy. It dispels falsehood, lies and darkness and exposes inconsistency and deception.

When traditional Africans swear by their elders, parents, ancestors or by God, they are appealing to the ultimate source of truth. By mentioning these names, they assert the certainty, veracity and truthfulness of what is being said. They may even be compelled to do something that they would much rather not do simply because they swore an oath using a trusted name.

The gospels and Pauline epistles introduce this same element into Christian ethics when they speak of doing things in the name of the Lord, and extend that to cover everything we do: "Whatever you do, whether in word or deed, do it all in the name of the Lord Jesus" (Col 3:17). All that we say and do must be rooted in the nature of God who is true. We should have the same reverence for the name of Christ that traditional Africans attach to the names of elders and ancestors.

God is faithful

God is faithful (Deut 7:9; Ps 36:5; 119:90). In Hebrew, the word "faithfulness" expresses "the total dependability of [God's] character or promises".[21] Yet this is the most questioned attribute of God. Many have abandoned their faith in God because they could not reconcile the faithfulness of God with the evils that have befallen them. That is why traditional African women would sing songs of lamentation, indirectly questioning the faithfulness of God. God does not take offence when people do this when they are mourning. This is a peaceful channel for expressing a complaint that could not be handled through direct confrontation. In the same way, wives sing songs reflecting their displeasure with their husbands.

Sometimes Africans try to manipulate God and bargain with him in order to get the best out of him. Some Africans think that if they offer God a lot of beer and get him drunk, they can get what they want. Such an approach shows a lack of confidence in the faithfulness and dependability of God.

It takes a lot to convince people that God is still faithful, even after calamity has struck. But in the face of evil, suffering, disease, death and the contingencies of life, we need a God who can be relied on, one who is faithful, true, reliable and dependable. Human beings need an anchor that holds life together and gives it meaning and purpose.

God's Laws

Our study of God's attributes has given us a very clear idea that God is holy and righteous. All of these attributes together feed into God's universal order, which consists of 1) universal physical laws and 2) universal moral laws, which apply to all moral creatures.

God's universal physical laws

At creation, God set in place universal physical laws that uphold the physical and material order. These laws were established by God's powerful word and they demonstrate his creative power, which is rooted in his sovereign power. God's spoken word provides the physical order to all of creation.

God's universal physical laws are temporal. At the end of the age when Christ establishes his kingdom, they will be destroyed along with the created old order.

God's universal moral laws

God's universal moral laws are not part of creation but transcend it. They are rooted in God's moral nature, character and attributes, and thus they are eternal and universal. They are intended to govern the behaviour of human beings whom God made in his image to reflect his character.

The Hebrew word translated as "law" is *torah*. It means "teaching" or "instruction". God's law is thus teaching or instruction on how we should live. That is why the Bible contains sayings like, "My son, do not forget my teaching (*torah*), but keep my commands in your heart, for they will prolong your life many years and bring you peace and prosperity" (Prov 3:1–2). This law supersedes all traditional moral codes by renewing and transforming them. It is thus the responsibility of the Christian community to ensure that God's moral laws are translated into moral and social behaviour. Christian communal values have greater impact upon society than individual ethics.

Why a Right Understanding of God Matters

Despite much academic talk about the role of God in African Traditional Religion, the Supreme God is the remotest of all beings in traditional thought. There is no concept of him as Immanuel, God with us. All that remains after the fall is a rudimentary knowledge of his existence. Traditional worship and spirituality focus far more on spirit beings and spirit powers.

Given this lack of knowledge of the true God revealed in Jesus Christ, it is not surprising that some Africans think that they can blame God for the existence of evil. But our study of God's moral character and of the moral order of the universe that he has created shows that it is impossible to associate him with sin, wrongdoing or evil. God's holiness, goodness, righteousness, justice, truth and faithfulness make it impossible for him to sin or to be evil. We must look elsewhere to trace the origin of sin and evil.

But where should we look? If evil and sin are not traceable to God, where did they begin? With creation? The prevalence of evil and sin certainly makes some people think that they are part of original creation. Were they created by God or by lesser gods? If so, what do we do about them? That will be the topic of the next chapter.

4

CREATION: GOOD OR BAD?

If the concept of God is fuzzy for some traditional Africans (and for other groups around the world) that of creation is even fuzzier. There are all sorts of competing accounts of how the world came to be and of how sin and evil came to play such a prominent part in it.

The View of World Religions

Different groups have different understandings of the world. Those who are atheists and materialists deny the existence of God, and thus also deny the very idea of creation. They hold that everything that exists evolved from some pre-existing matter, and that life has no purpose or meaning. They thus define evil and sin as whatever causes us discomfort.

At the opposite extreme are the polytheists, who believe in many gods, any one or group of whom could have been involved in various aspects of creation. In some versions of the creation story, particularly in ancient Greece, the gods bring forth creatures through mating and birth. In these stories, it is often the lesser gods who introduce evil and sin because of conflicts between them.

The ancient Greeks were polytheists, but they were also philosophers. In their thinking about the origin of the world, they proposed two eternal principles. The first was the existence of eternal, pre-existing matter that has no form or shape. The second was an eternal principle of organization, which gives form, structure or shape to things. When these two eternal principles of matter and form come together, things are brought into being. In this view, God is not so much a creator as a craftsman, using rational thinking to unite eternal matter with an eternal form or shape. In other words, God is the organizer of reality, not its creator. This view limits God, for he is not seen as the Sovereign Lord of the universe.

In later Greek thought, forms or ideas were thought to be divine and good, while material things were thought to be evil:

> The source of goodness and fulfilment lay in the formal order of life, and the source of evil in the material, chaotic elements of reality. The world of space and time, of material changing things, of bodily desires and passions, and personal love, of death and decay, seemed therefore to the later Greek mind to be a world of evil. This evil is, moreover, necessary and unconquerable.[22]

This Greek belief that the source of evil is embedded in the material creation was accepted by some early Christians who became convinced that they must thus reject everything to do with this world. They became hermits and denied themselves food and clothing in an attempt to avoid being contaminated by evil. But on this view, evil can never be overcome in this world simply because the world itself is material, and thus evil.

Other groups like Hindus and Buddhists hold to pantheism, believing that everything that exists is a part of God, so that there is no separation between God and creation. "Creatures are made, not out of matter, but are out of God, for creaturely existence is a manifestation of the divine."[23] Creation is an emanation or overflow from God, its source, and the material world is a prison because it hinders people from recognizing their true status and becoming divine themselves. Thus creaturely existence is viewed as illusory (not real) and as evil, for "what is not God, then, is neither real nor good."[24] Just like the Greeks, Eastern religions see evil as an eternal principle embedded in creation, which cannot be eradicated. They too view the material world as evil and to be shunned.

The View of African Religions

African traditional religious beliefs, as enshrined in numerous creation stories, fall somewhere between those of the Greeks and Eastern religions and have elements of both. African polytheism believes that there are many gods. While the Supreme Being is said to have created the world, lesser gods or spirit beings were also involved.

African stories provide various answers to the question, "How did God create?" When we played God as children, we would use clay by the river to shape all kinds of creatures. Our actions conformed to one set of traditional beliefs that see God as a craftsman like a potter or carpenter. Our clay symbolized the pre-existing matter that he was presumed to have used to do his work of creation. Other traditions hold that the Supreme Being created humans, animals, birds, mountains, rivers, oceans, heaven and earth and so on out of nothing.

For Africans, the origin of creation is shrouded in mystery. They see no need to go beyond this mystery to find answers, for in African philosophy and religion, mystery is often assumed to be the starting point of knowledge. It is a given reality. God is the Creator – Africans feel no need to dissect the details of how he created.

According to African Traditional Religion, the Supreme Being delegated some of his powers of creation to lesser gods, some of whom misused these powers and created things that were opposed to God or to human beings. Was evil created by these beings, or is it an eternal principle in the universe? The answer is not clear. African believers would say that this too is best left as a mystery. What is clear is that evil is associated with lesser beings and spirits.

All the lesser beings are feared because they have power to do both good and evil. Moreover, they are treacherous and work against God and human beings. Some, like the deceiving divinity Esu in Yoruba religion, are personifications of evil.

God does not seem to be powerful enough to contain evil and its perpetrators. For this reason, humans are left to fend for themselves by soliciting protection and preservation from the lesser gods.

The Christian View

There are some striking similarities between the Christian conception of God and creation and that of African Traditional Religion, which means that traditional beliefs can serve as a starting point to introduce God's special revelation in the Holy Scriptures and Jesus Christ.

First, Africans and Christians agree that God created the universe. It is not an emanation or an extension of God, as Eastern religions teach, but exists as something distinct from its Creator. He is separate from and transcendent to his created universe.

Second, Africans and Christians also agree that the process by which God created is mysterious, and we accept this mystery as something that we do not need to have explained.

Where Christianity and African Traditional Religion part company is that Christianity insists that God created everything – he did not leave parts of the work to lesser gods. Moreover, he did not create the world out of existing materials but out of nothing. There was no pre-existing material. He is the source of everything that exists, and is not merely an organizer of existing natural forces. Everything that exists came into existence through his word of power. God's act of creation is from non-existence to existence, from nothing to something.

Everything that God created is good (Gen 1:13). Given the attributes of God outlined in the previous section, he could not have created something that was evil. But evil exists. Where does it come from? In answering this question, African religious thought is quite similar to the teaching of the Bible as regards the origin of evil and sin. In both traditions, God did his work of creation and created some powerful lesser beings who rebelled against him and disobeyed his instructions. By doing this, they brought evil into being, with devastating consequences for humans and creation.

But once again Christianity and African Traditional Religion diverge radically when it comes to what this state of affairs means. Traditional religion succumbs to a vague fatalism and assumes that nothing can be done about evil, beyond trying to avert it through rituals, sacrifices and offerings.[25]

By contrast, Christianity says that we do not have to passively accept the ways things are. God himself has taken steps to deal with the problem of Satan, evil and sin. He did this through the work of Christ on the cross, his resurrection and his cosmic rule over the universe. We will look at this in more detail in the next chapter.

Why a Right Understanding of Creation Matters

African Christians can confidently assert that this world is not dominated by fate or evil and is not meaningless. It is ruled by a loving Sovereign Lord. Thus we should not simply accept that evil is inevitable and tolerate sin. Instead, recognizing that creation is good, we should seek to maintain that goodness by striving to create just, participatory and sustainable societies based on God's moral laws. We should work to eradicate poverty, hunger, disease, wars and many vices and sins.

African Christians also need to know where evil and sin fit into creation. In Africa, we are enslaved by evil spirits, for the spirit power embedded in our traditional religion is powerless in the face of evil and sin. The most we can seek to do is to manipulate this spirit power. But Christianity delivers people from such enslavement. The victory of Jesus Christ on the cross signals the total conquest of Satan and his demonic forces. Christ has overcome evil and sin both in nature in general and in human nature.

5
EVIL, SIN AND FREE WILL

I have mentioned that as a child I used to wonder why God had not created a world free of sin and evil, Satan and demons. At that time, I did not recognize that such questioning ultimately blames God for the existence of evil.

Many years later, as a professor at a seminary, I found that the same questions I used to raise as a child were regularly raised by my students. They saw structural evil embedded in creation and were aware of its dominance in human affairs throughout history. They recognized that this raises serious questions about God's goodness and omnipotence. Why does he not eradicate evil once and for all?

I offered biblical answers, but my African theological students were not satisfied. It was not that they were not hearing my answers, but that what they were hearing did not make sense to them. My talk of a Sovereign Lord who is holy and perfect and who created the world good did not match their perception that the world is filled with evil, wickedness, afflictions and calamities. They were far more inclined to attribute fateful events to witchcraft than to God, and to see evil spiritual powers as almost on a par with God.

Africans are not alone in having difficulty fitting the Christian answers to the problem of evil into their own world view. Many Western scholars have had the same problem. They have tried to reduce the biblical teachings on the origin of evil and sin to myths or fables, teaching moral lessons. With their world view dominated by rationalism and scepticism, they cannot conceive of Adam and Eve as historical figures or of the garden of Eden as a real place.

The African world view, by contrast, is not dominated by rationalism, secularism, or scientism. Rather, Africans tend to be interested in accommodation, domestication and adaptation. Their problem is not disbelief or scepticism but too much belief, and an unwillingness to accept that they have to choose between a Christian explanation for the origin of sin and evil and the explanation offered by African Traditional Religion.

The Nature of Evil

A very important starting point when thinking about the nature of evil is to recognize that it is not eternal. Only God is eternal and omnipotent (Isa 44:6). Evil itself has no divine eternal nature. It is not a power that is equal and opposite to God.

As we saw in an earlier chapter, the Bible makes it clear that God's character is holy and that he cannot be associated with evil. It is impossible for Eternal Goodness and Eternal Perfection to create evil or think evil. A logical consequence of this was brought out by the great African scholar St. Augustine when he said that "evil is not a substance".[26] The point he was making is that evil is not something that God has created. Rather, it is a "perversion of a nature that is essentially good". Evil is a distortion of God's good creation that "thwarts continuously and seriously the potential goodness of creation, destroying alike its intelligibility and meaning and making life as we experience it so threatening, so full of sorrow, suffering and apparent pointlessness."[27]

Evil and Free Will

How then did evil enter into God's good creation? How can we explain the rise of something that had not existed before? The only possible answer is that it arose because one of the gifts God gave to his creation was freedom. He created beings who were free to make real choices.

When God created the universe, he made it out of nothing, using only the word of his power. In the same way, the good creatures he had made created evil out of nothing when they used their free will to make a bad choice.

Of course, we can ask why God gave his creatures free will in the first place. But we cannot answer that question. God who is infinite, eternal and unchangeable in his wisdom chose to create them that way. We are in no position to advise God on what he should be doing. All we know is that they were created free in order to glorify his name.

It may be helpful to summarize what I have been saying:

- Evil is not an essential or necessary part of our existence. We were created good.
- Evil came only after God's act of creation.
- Evil is the misuse of good things by putting them to bad use.
- God created good beings and gave them the freedom to choose to serve God or themselves.
- Evil arose when these beings chose to serve themselves and not the good God who created them.
- In order to understand this, we need to look closely at the story of creation and fall.

Why We Were Created

Unless faced with calamity or tragedy, we do not often ask ourselves, "What is our purpose in life?" In fact, many humans could not answer this question. They simply live from day to day, without any awareness of the purpose for which they were created. This in itself reflects our fallen condition; we have lost our way and do not know why we exist.

Even Christians may be challenged if asked why God created human beings. Did he create us because he was lonely or because he needed fellowship with other beings? No, for there was perfect love and fellowship among the members of the Trinity for all eternity (John 17:5, 24). He had no need of other companions.

So why did he create us? Maybe the best way to approach this question is to ask another question: "Are creatures brought into being ... to please God ... or to please themselves; for the fulfilment of God's purposes or for the fulfilment of their own happiness?"[28] That question we can answer: God made us for his own purposes. He says that he created his children "for my glory" (Isa 43:7) and Paul reminds us that we are to live "for the praise of his glory" (Eph 1:12). As the Westminster Catechism says, "Man's chief end is to glorify God, and to enjoy him forever."[29]

Because God created us so that we can worship (praise, glorify) him, serve him and live in obedience and loyalty to him, we should be living this way all the days of our life. We should not need to ask why we should love and worship God, but should love him because of his intrinsic worth. God is worthy to be loved, worshipped, served and obeyed for his own sake.[30] He deserves all glory because he is the Creator who made all things. The Apostle John states: "You are worthy, our Lord and God, to receive glory and honour and power, for you created all things, and by your will they were created and have their being" (Rev 4:11). Jesus quoted the Jewish statement of faith, the *Shema*, when he said: "Hear, O Israel: the Lord our God, the Lord is one. Love the Lord your God with all your heart and with all your soul and with all your mind and with all your strength. The second is this: 'Love your neighbour as yourself.' There is no commandment greater than these" (Mark 12:29–31).

Our Original Condition

Our present human condition reflects the impact of the fall into sin. But what were we made to be? It is only when we know this that we can know and appreciate God's work of redemption in restoring us to our original state through the death of Jesus Christ.

Genesis tells us what we were made to be when it quotes God as saying: "Let us make mankind in our image, in our likeness" (1:26). The words "image" and "likeness" indicate that we were created to be similar to God but not identical to him. We are to represent God in this world.[31]

Let me explain this concept using the new translation of the Bible into the Gyong language of Nigeria. In that translation, the Hebrew word translated "image" in English Bibles is translated as *shou Num*, which literally means "a being of God". This implies not that human beings come from God, but rather that human nature is God-like. Our nature is similar to that of God. Given that God's nature is real and true, that is what we were intended to be like. He sets the standard for every aspect of our being. In other words, in our total being, we are to take after the total being of God (although we can never be the same as God and are not simply an emanation of God).

The Hebrew word translated "likeness" in English Bibles is translated as *mnet Num* in Gyong. This word refers to a resemblance to God that focuses on our outward form, rather than on our inner nature.

It is sometimes suggested that Jesus Christ represents what we were created to be. After all, in passages like Romans 5:12–19 he is referred to as the Second Adam and Christians are commanded to put on the "new self", that is Jesus Christ (Eph 4:24).[32]

However, it is important to stress the marked difference between Jesus Christ and the first Adam. The first Adam was never the revelation of God in the same way that Jesus Christ is (John 1:18). Jesus came from God. He does not just bear his image and likeness, but shares his exact nature. Thus in Hebrews, Jesus is described as the "exact representation of his [God's] being" (Heb 1:3), and the Apostle Paul refers to him as "the image of the invisible God" (Col 1:15). He is the complete revelation of God.

God's First Covenant with Adam and Eve

As we read the story of what happened in the garden of Eden, we can see that God dealt with Adam and Eve on the basis of 1) his moral nature and character; 2) the moral order of creation, and 3) his moral law for moral creatures.

Adam was on probation in the garden of Eden, to see whether he would live up to the image of God that he represented. God expressed his moral law through making a covenant with Adam that would apply to every human being, for Adam was the head of the entire human race. This initial covenant, made before the fall, contained the following commands (Gen 1:28–29; 2:15–17):

- populate the earth (Gen 1:28)
- subdue the earth
- exercise dominion over animals
- care for the garden of Eden and enjoy its fruits

- do not eat the fruit of the tree of the knowledge of good and evil, on penalty of death.

Adam was on probation, and unfortunately he failed the test.

What Happened in Eden

The story of the fall begins with the appearance of the Tempter in Genesis 3. The visible tempter was the serpent (3:1). But the real and invisible Tempter was Satan himself. He only used the serpent as a means to achieve his purpose.

Who was Satan?

Humans are not the only beings to whom God gave free will. He also gave free will to his angels, who are created spiritual beings with moral judgement and high intelligence, but without physical bodies.[33] Both Satan and demons are angels who were created good, but who used their free will to sin. They lost their place in heaven and the privilege of serving God.

> **THE TEMPTER**
> Satan inside the Serpent
>
> A created spirit being
> A proud heart
> A sinful attitude
> The father of lies
> A murderer from the beginning
>
> Genesis 3; Isaiah 14; Ezekiel 28

What was the temptation?

All kinds of stories are told about what happened in Eden. Some argue about what type of fruit was involved, and whether it was an apple or an apricot. Some argue that the sin was the sexual seduction of Adam by Eve. Some dismiss the entire story as a myth lacking any historical basis, arguing about whether its purpose is only to teach morality or whether it represents an attempt to find answers to the ultimate realities of life like evil and sin.

I will not discuss any of these theories here, but will instead focus on what the Bible says. There, we are told that when the Tempter approached Eve, he began with a question, "Did God really say …?", and then challenged her account of what God had said, saying "You will not certainly die" (3:1–4). In effect, the Tempter was saying that God is a liar. He was attacking the very nature of God as true, holy, righteous, wise and faithful. He was undermining Eve's faith in the authority and power of God's word. He denied that God is the ultimate lawgiver and judge by removing the sword of the law and the sting of death.

Next, the Tempter sowed more mistrust by implying that God is not perfect and good. He questioned God's motive for commanding Adam and Eve not to eat of the tree of the knowledge of good and evil. He made the command seem an unnecessary burden because it limited their freedom. Having deflected Eve's attention away from God's command and its consequences, the Tempter encouraged Eve to eat the fruit by holding out the three benefits eating would bring: 1) wisdom – "your eyes will be opened"; 2) "you will be like God"; and 3) you will gain knowledge of "good and evil" (Gen 3:5). But these "benefits" were not what they appeared to be. All the Tempter's offers were counterfeits.

> **THE TEMPTER'S CHARGES**
>
> God is a liar
> God cannot be trusted
> God does not seek our ultimate good
>
> Genesis 3:4-5

The first counterfeit offered was wisdom. The Tempter encouraged Eve to forget that God is the only possessor of wisdom and the one who gives wisdom. Instead, she was told that in denying them the right to eat the fruit, God was denying them wisdom. But wisdom does not come by eating fruit but only from God, who is Eternal Wisdom. Eve was being encouraged to use her free will to prefer human wisdom to the true wisdom of God.

The second counterfeit was a reformulation of what it means to be made in the image of God. Eve was already "in the image of God" and represented him. So when the Tempter said "you will be like God", all he could offer was a counterfeit likeness. Instead of becoming more like God, sinful human beings would actually become less like God – although they might seem more like gods in their own eyes.

The third counterfeit, knowledge of good and evil, was actually knowledge of sin and death. Eve had been created good and thus had no knowledge of what evil is like. The Tempter suggests that this is something that God knows and she does not, implying that God is selfishly keeping it from her. What Eve failed to recognize is that God's knowledge of evil is only external – he knows about it, but is not tainted by it, for there is no trace of evil in his nature. However, Eve's knowledge of evil would be personal and would contaminate her.

Through his attack on Eve, the Tempter was indirectly attacking God by trying to thwart his purpose in creation. He was questioning the entire moral and physical order that God had established in Eden, in which human beings, made in the image of God, tended the tree of life and the tree of the knowledge of good and evil, and obeyed the commands in Genesis 1:29–30 and 2:15–17, 24. The Tempter wanted to spit in God's face by advocating lawlessness, rebellion, disobedience and immorality, and he encouraged creatures to rise up against their Maker. He was throwing down the gauntlet to the Sovereign Lord of the universe (see also Isa 14:12–14).

The Fall and God's Second Covenant with Adam and Eve

The first covenant God made with Adam and Eve was terminated by their rebellion and disobedience when they listened to the Tempter and ate the forbidden fruit of the tree of the knowledge of good and evil. Their action had devastating consequences not only in the moral realm but also in the physical realm. God's creatures had chosen to adopt a moral law that was contrary to God's law of goodness. And moral values or virtues are not neutral and inert; they affect the physical order and institutions. Thus evil led to both spiritual and physical weakness, suffering and death. All of these are the by-products of human sin and were not part of God's original creation. These results should not have been unexpected, for God had warned Adam and Eve about the consequence of choosing to disobey his law (Gen 2:15–17).

The first covenant had been broken, and so God made a second covenant with Adam and Eve (Gen 3:14–21). This covenant, which was given as punishment for sin, sets out the conditions that will dominate human life until the curse of sin is lifted when Christ establishes his kingdom (Rev 20–22):[34]

- the serpent, the tool that Satan used, is cursed
- Satan is judged
- Eve is punished with painful childbirth and subjection to her husband
- the ground is cursed on account of Adam's sin
- Adam has to work very hard in order to eat
- death is a reality.

One of the major punishments was God's curse on creation. It is because the physical universe was cursed by God that we live in a world in which our lives are affected by natural evils. The physical laws that God created when the world began were intended to ensure its and our well-being. But these laws no longer apply in the same way. Now we live in a world where earthquakes, floods, volcanic eruptions and the like spread devastation.

Some humans have no idea that this world is not as it was intended to be. Consequently they can offer no solution to the problem of sin and evil. It is only when we recognize that these are later additions, not part of the original creation, that we can even have hope that they can be overcome, and be motivated to look for solutions, while trusting in God, the only one who can restore creation to its original perfect state.

The power of Satan and his demonic and spiritual hosts is not only manifested in a fallen creation but also in human nature, societies and communities. His power is behind all forms of evil and sin in human society. Adam and Eve's sin gave his forces a foothold in every human society. The more people sin, the stronger is Satan's power and the more secure his foothold in human lives.

Why Understanding Free Will Matters

Where evil predominates, fatalism takes over. Many in Africa have resigned themselves to living with anxiety and fear. They assume that their destiny has already been settled by powers they cannot control and that everything is hopeless and meaningless. God does not seem to be active in protecting them from these powers and so they search for spiritual powers that will offer protection and security.

Where life is dominated by anxiety and fear, we need to emphasize the sovereignty and power of God. We know that evil is not an essential part of the world that God created, and thus we know that it can be overcome. And that is what God has done. The Sovereign Lord, who is Love, has made a way to redeem his fallen creation and eradicate the scourge of evil and sin through his final revelation in Jesus Christ. All menacing spirit powers and spirit beings have been defeated by the cross of Christ.

The gospel of Jesus Christ is the message of hope that God has overcome evil and dealt with it decisively on the cross. The law of goodness revealed in the cross of Jesus Christ is the basis for challenging sin and evil in the world. God had dealt a death blow to the law of sin and evil.

Even though our societies are infected by moral and spiritual decadence and corruption, there is hope. Repentance and revival will bring healing, cleansing and restoration of peace: "If my people, who are called by my name, will humble themselves and pray and seek my face and turn from their wicked ways, then I will hear from heaven and I will forgive their sin and will heal their land" (2 Chr 7:14).

6

THE POWER OF TEMPTATION

A certain servant often complained that he had to work hard and blamed Adam and Eve for all his suffering. If they hadn't sinned, he wouldn't have had to work so hard.

His master eventually grew tired of this particular complaint and decided to test him. He told the servant that he would be going on a long journey and would leave the care of the house in his hands. He gave the servant specific instructions regarding a container in the centre of the parlour. He was never to touch it or open it.

For the first few days after his master's departure, the servant did his chores as usual without paying much attention to the container. But then, he began to wonder what was inside it. As the days passed, he thought more and more about this. The desire to know what was in it grew stronger, and became an obsession. Some days, he would stand and look at the container for hours.

Gradually he moved from watching and wondering to desiring to touch. But he dared not do so. His master's command rang in his ears each time he thought about touching it. But with time, he began to hear it less, and one day, summoning up all his courage, he reached out a finger and touched the container.

To his amazement nothing happened. All was normal. The fear of touching the container was gone, but his desire to know what was inside it grew. Was it something valuable that he could steal? His desire to know the answer consumed him, so that he could not rest. Not knowing was driving him crazy!

Eventually, he could bear it no longer. He walked up to the container, touched it, picked it up and quietly and carefully opened it. What would he find inside?

As the lid came off, an enormous rat leaped out of the container and ran across the room. All that the container held was the rat and a supply of food and water for it!

Desperate to recapture the rat before his master returned, the servant started to chase it around the room. Just at that moment, his master returned.

The servant discovered that he could no longer blame all his troubles on Adam and Eve!

The Power of Temptation

All human beings face temptations. These temptations do not come from God. The Apostle James states this plainly: "When tempted, no one should say; 'God is tempting me.' For God cannot be tempted by evil, nor does he tempt anyone" (Jas 1:13). Temptations come from Satan, who seeks to deceive us just as he deceived Eve. That is why the writer of the book of Hebrews speaks of "sin's deceitfulness" (Heb 3:13).

In the first stage of temptation, evil seeks to deceive the mind; in the second, it entices our emotions; and in the third, it leads us to decide to sin. But evil does not become sin unless we accept it and allow ourselves to be dragged away and enticed by our own evil desires (Jas 1:14). That is why the Apostle John warns us, "Do not love the world or anything in the world … the lust of the flesh, the lust of their eyes and the pride of life" (1 John 2:15–16). Both Satan and the world tempt us to sin.

Even the strongest of Christians are often challenged by temptation. If we think we are too mature in Christ to fall, we should remember what Eve was like. She was God's perfect creation, still bearing his uncorrupted image. She was perfect, holy and sinless. Nevertheless, she fell into sin because she succumbed to the deceptions of the Evil One.

If Eve fell, so can we. We have an enemy who operates subtly, secretly and undercover, and who knows when, where and how to strike, whether in public or in private. We need to be vigilant at all times. Our

Lord told us to "watch and pray" against the hour of temptation (Matt 26:41). As John Owen says, "Temptation especially assaults us in times of prosperity, indifference, success, or self-confidence. We must fortify our heart against the approaches of temptation, especially during these more vulnerable times."[35]

We can learn more about how the Tempter operates by looking at what happened to Eve in the Garden of Eden when she failed to recognize his lies for what they were.

The Context of Temptation

Adam and Eve were created by God in his own image. They thus shared some of the attributes of God, including his freedom from sin and freedom of choice. They were not machines, who had no option but to obey God. They could freely choose to obey or disobey him.

But freedom is not true freedom unless there is an opportunity to choose. That is why God gave Adam and Eve such an opportunity. When he placed them in the garden, he also placed there the tree of the knowledge of good and evil and instructed them not to eat its fruit, on pain of death (Gen 2:15–17).

The Instrument of Temptation

Lies were the instrument the Tempter used to attack God's truth, wisdom and goodness. All that he offered Eve was false or counterfeit. When we accept a lie or counterfeit knowledge, it leads to the development of a sinful attitude. So when Eve accepted the Tempter's lies, they led her to change her mind about the law of God and God himself.

Rebellion and Disobedience

When he first encountered Eve, the Tempter simply asked her about God's command. She stepped into dangerous territory when she misquoted what God had said, adding her own words, "And you must not touch it" (Gen 3:3). God had merely said that they should not eat the fruit.

In the previous chapter, we saw how the Tempter then set about offering Eve counterfeit blessings if she would disobey God's command. She failed to recognize the danger. Instead, she allowed herself to see the fruit of the tree in a new, captivating light.

The evil desire to disobey God's explicit instruction did not arise from Eve's original nature, for she was perfect, holy and sinless. She could easily have rejected all the lies of the Tempter if she had wanted to do so. But instead she listened to his slander of God, his lies about the effects of eating the fruit, and of her own free will she allowed herself to be seduced by what she saw and heard. This is how the Tempter often works, trying to divert our attention from God to the mundane things of the world.

> **THE TEMPTER'S OFFERS**
>
> Immortality
> Opened eyes
> Being like God
> God-like knowledge
> Knowledge of good and evil
>
> Genesis 3:4-5

Genesis 3:6 tells us that there were three things in particular that caught her attention about the fruit of the tree of the knowledge of good and evil:

- It was "good for food". Eve was succumbing to greed. There was more than enough other food available in the garden, and she had no need to pick this forbidden fruit. By contrast, when Jesus was tempted in the desert, he refused to turn stones into bread even though he was hungry (Matt 11:1–4). He resisted the temptations of greed; Eve did not.

- It was "pleasing to the eye". This is the type of desire that the Apostle John calls "the lust of their eyes" (1 John 2:16). Jesus, too, faced this temptation when he was shown "all the kingdoms of the world and their splendour" (Matt 4:8). It was not seeing the beauty that was wrong, but the evil desire that arose from this seeing. Beauty was not meant to be used as an excuse for doing wrong.

- It was "desirable for gaining wisdom". This element appealed to what John calls "the pride of life" (1 John 2:16), that is, the selfishness and self-centredness that the Tempter tried to exploit when he took Jesus to the temple and urged him to show off in order to demonstrate the miraculous saving power of God (Matt 4:5–7).

We will return to these issues when we look at the three pairs of root sins in the next section of this book. For the moment, let us concentrate on what Eve does: "she took some and ate" (Gen 3:6b). Up until this moment, evil had simply been an external idea floated by Satan that Eve had allowed to enter her mind. But she accepted this evil idea and thought it through in the full freedom of her mind. Then she chose to act upon it. In doing this, she appropriated evil and gave birth to sin. The image of God in her was shattered. She ceased to be sinless; instead, sin became her second nature.

This is one way to distinguish between evil and sin. Evil was merely an abstract idea until Eve acted on it. Sin is physical, and not merely an idea. Sin is the incarnation of evil.

The Consequences of the Fall

The Tempter told Eve that after she ate the fruit, her status and nature would change. Did this happen? Did Adam and Eve receive what they hoped for when they ate the fruit of the tree of the knowledge of good and evil? Did they become like God as promised by the Tempter?

Yes, they became like gods because "their eyes were opened" and they did "become wise" – but the wisdom they acquired was only their own independent and personal wisdom, which cut them off from God's eternal and holy wisdom. Yes, they got to know both "good and evil" – but it was in the form of their own good and evil in opposition to God.

No, they did not become like God who is Eternal Goodness. He knows evil, but only as an external idea; Adam and Eve now knew it both internally and externally. They lost their original perfect and holy nature and became evil internally. They exchanged the image of the eternal God for their own mortality. For the rest of their lives, they would be haunted by sin, ruin and death.

When Adam and Eve's eyes were opened, they suddenly became self-conscious. They were no longer caught up in the worship of God and the work he had given them to do. Looking at each other, "they realized they were naked" (Gen 3:7) and sowed fig leaves together to cover themselves.

Their shame at their nakedness was also a sign of their new sin-consciousness. They knew that they had disobeyed God. Ashamed at what they had done, they hid from him.

But when God appeared in the garden, their shame was overshadowed by an even stronger emotion – guilt. They recognized that they had become transgressors, lawbreakers, who deserved judgement, condemnation and punishment for their sin against the holy God, their Maker.

Adam and Eve's sin not only had disastrous effects on their own nature, but affected all their descendants, who now have to live with inherited guilt and inherited corruption.

Because Adam and Eve were our first parents, the representative heads of humanity, their fall meant the fall of the entire human race. This concept troubles many Western theologians and philosophers who are steeped in rationalism and scepticism. Some of them argue that it is unjust for the sin of Adam and Eve to affect all their descendents. True, Adam and Eve abused their freedom and choice and sinned, but why should their guilt and deserved punishment also afflict their "innocent" descendents?

This question makes little sense to Africans because we understand the importance of our genealogy or lineage. This is part of our belief in kinship values. Everyone with whom we share a common ancestor is our brother or sister. Physical characteristics and elements of character are passed down from parents to children through the ages. So are behaviours, both good and evil. Skills in witchcraft, divination and other mysterious matters are seen as hereditary. So Africans have no difficulty in accepting that all human beings inherit a sinful nature from Adam.

We do not see the need to offer a scientific explanation for this reality. For traditional Africans, reality goes beyond biology and lies in the spirit realm. Original sin is easily understood in terms of the spirit power of the ancestors over their descendents.

But that gives rise to another question. If we are fallen and corrupted because of our ancestor's sin, why are we still blamed for our own sins and wrongdoings? This is a good question, and the best answer is that all human beings inherited two things from Adam's sin, namely guilt and corruption.[36]

Inherited guilt

We are all guilty before God. This is our legal position both because our nature is now sinful and because we have committed specific sins. Some theologians refer to this condition as original sin.

Adam represented all humans at the test in the garden of Eden. The Apostle Paul explains the effects of Adam's sin upon his descendents as follows: "Sin entered the world through one man, and death through sin, and in this way death came to all people, because all sinned" (Rom 5:12). He is saying that in the sin of Adam, everyone sinned. We were all complicit in his disobedience. Paul repeats the same point in Romans 5:18–19: "one trespass resulted in condemnation for all people … through the disobedience of the one man the many were made sinners (Rom 5:18–19).

Rationalists and scientists are baffled by this, but it is a deep spiritual principle that is beyond our comprehension. As Paul reminds us:

> The Spirit searches all things, even the deep things of God. For who knows a person's thoughts except that person's own spirit within? In the same way, no one knows the thoughts of God except the Spirit of God. We have not received the spirit of the world but the Spirit who is from God, that we may understand what God has freely given us. This is what we speak, not in words taught us by human wisdom but in words taught by the Spirit, explaining spiritual realities with Spirit-taught words. The person without the Spirit does not accept the things that come from the Spirit of God but considers them foolishness, and cannot understand them, because they are discerned only through the Spirit. (1 Cor 2:10–14)

Because of our inherited guilt (and our own sinful acts) we are all guilty sinners, deserving of God's judgement and punishment. Our only hope is in Christ, who can remove our guilt.

Inherited corruption

Not only are we all guilty because of Adam's sin, but we also all now have a sinful disposition or tendency to sin. King David was well aware of this, saying "Surely, I was sinful at birth, sinful from the time my mother conceived me" (Ps 51:5). A later psalm reads, "Even from birth the wicked go astray; from the womb they are wayward, spreading lies" (Ps 58:3).

Our inherited corruption affects the totality of our being. Its effects are felt by all, including those who believe in Jesus Christ. Even the Apostle Paul felt it. He describes his situation in these terms: "So I find this law at work: Although I want to do good, evil is right there with me. ... I see another law at work in me, waging war against the law of my mind and making me a prisoner of the law of sin at work within me" (Rom 7:21-23). Later, he refers to this as "the law of sin and death" (Rom 8:2).

The inherited corruption in our natures expresses itself in hostility towards God. "The mind governed by the flesh is hostile to God. It does not submit to God's law, nor can it do so" (Rom 8:7).

God's Judgement and Punishment

People are happy to think of God as their Father, but they complain when he punishes sin. They want God to be kind and caring and take human weaknesses and limitations into account, rather than acting "harshly". After all, it can be difficult to keep his laws. We like the idea of a benevolent God, full of love, mercy, forgiveness and kindness. But we hate to think of a God who judges and punishes wrongdoing. Yet Christianity teaches that God is both loving and just. So after Adam and Eve sinned, God took decisive action that affected the entire human race.

The first thing God did was to confront Adam and Eve in the Garden of Eden. But when they heard him coming, they ran away and hid among the trees. They knew they had done wrong and were afraid to meet God.

So God called out to Adam, "Where are you?" Adam was summoned into the presence of God and asked to account for his behaviour. Then God as the lawgiver announces his verdict: Adam, Eve and the serpent are guilty of the sin of disobedience. He then pronounces judgement on them.

God's judgement is given in the form of a curse, that is, a word of power that brings destruction or punishment on the person or thing cursed. When God invokes a curse his words carry spirit power and have spiritual consequences as well as physical effects. His curse on the primary actors in the garden of Eden affected them and all that belonged to them – their environment, possessions, inheritance and descendents. This too does not surprise adherents of African Traditional Religion, for they know the power of curses and their effects on both the spiritual and physical realms.

Nothing we can do can lift God's curse. The only thing that can nullify it is the cross of Christ. Jesus took God's curse to the cross and cancelled it. There he dealt with the root of sin. However, even though Christ has broken the power of this curse, its effects will still be with us until his second coming when he will establish his rule over the new heaven and new earth. In the interim, while we wait for our final redemption, we are to apply the power of the cross in our lives. We will deal with how to do this later in the book.

God's judgement on the serpent

God first pronounces judgement on the serpent. His judgement has two parts, reflecting the fact that the serpent as an animal was only an instrument used as camouflage by the real Tempter. But that did not excuse it from punishment.

The serpent as an animal was cursed with being hated more than "all livestock and all wild animals" and was told that it would crawl on its belly and "eat dust" (Gen 3:14).

The Tempter concealed within the serpent was cursed with enduring enmity between him and the woman, and between his offspring (Satan) and the woman's offspring (Christ). The latter would crush Satan's head, whereas Satan would only be able to strike at his heel (Gen 3:15).

God's judgement on Eve

God next punishes Eve for being deceived by the serpent. The fact that she had been lied to and deceived could not be used as an excuse to escape God's judgement (Gen 3:13).

Eve's punishment was directed towards two important areas of her life. The first area was childbearing. Giving birth to children would become very painful. The second area was her relationship with her husband. She would long for and be dominated by him (Gen 3:16). Eve's descendants have paid a heavy price for her disobedience.

God's judgement on Adam

God punished Adam for two counts of wrongdoing: First, he listened to his wife and committed a wrong by eating the fruit of the tree, and second, he broke God's command, "You must not eat from the tree of the knowledge of good and evil" (Gen 2:17). Adam tried to escape responsibility by blaming God for giving him the wife who gave him the fruit to eat, but God would have none of it. Adam is personally responsible for his own sin. Being tempted is no excuse for giving in to sin, as the old hymn reminds us: "Yield not to temptation for yielding is sin."[37]

God served the following judgements on Adam: the ground was cursed because of Adam's sin; he would have to work very hard in order to get food to eat; the ground would produce thorns and thistles and he would eat plants of the field; he would return to the ground in death.

God's curse on the ground explains natural evil. When God created the heaven and earth, he put in place physical laws to govern the physical universe. All these laws worked in harmony with each other and with God's moral laws. However, when Satan and human beings broke the moral laws, the physical laws were also affected. Although physical laws are constant, there now crept in an element of disorder that causes chaos, conflict and a lack of harmony within creation. The Apostle Paul explains this phenomenon like this: "Creation was subjected to frustration, not by its own choice, but by the will of the one who subjected it, in hope that the creation itself will be liberated from its bondage to decay and brought into the freedom and glory of the children of God" (Rom 8:20–21).

The cross of Christ brings liberation to both humanity and the natural creation as both were adversely affected by Adam's sin. All the chaos and disharmony caused by the fall will be reconciled in the course of God's plan "to bring unity to all things in heaven and on earth under Christ" (Eph 1:10). When "the times reach their fulfilment" and that happens, chaos and disharmony will be replaced by reconciliation, restoration, regeneration and redemption of both humanity and the fallen creation. Ultimately, even death will be destroyed (1 Cor 15:26).

Living in exile

"Should you then seek great things for yourself? Do not seek them. For I will bring disaster on all people, declares the Lord" (Jer 45:5). The Tempter offered great things to Eve, but it all ended in disaster, shame, guilt, anxiety and fear. This has always been the bitter experience of humans when they ignore the advice of the author of Proverbs: "Do not be wise in your own eyes; fear the Lord and shun evil" (Prov 3:7).

Genesis 1 and 2 described how God shaped the earth to be a wonderful place for humans to live. But the one thing God did not give Adam and Eve was immortality. They might have been given this gift later, when he might have permitted them to eat of the tree of life in the garden of Eden, but once they had experienced evil, he made sure that they could never achieve it. He banished them from the garden and barred the way to the tree of life. If he had not done this, evil and sin would have become immortal and impossible to eradicate. There would then have been no hope for humanity, no redemption, no cross of Christ. But from now on the entire Bible unfolds the drama of God's plan to save us from the curse of evil and sin.

Adam and Eve were sent into exile outside the garden. And all of us still live in exile, with no access to paradise, the garden, the tree of life and the harmony of all creation. As exiles, we have to live with the curse, our weakness, suffering, and death. These are the wages earned by sin, the price of rebellion and disobedience.

But God was not a merciless judge. He had pity on Adam and Eve's helplessness as they cowered before him inadequately dressed in fig leaves. Their awareness of their nakedness was an awareness of their newly sinful nature. But God helped them to cover their nakedness by giving them "garments of skin" (Gen 3:21). In this act, God was declaring symbolically that he had a plan to redeem humanity and to deal with our sinful nature.

Conclusion

God's toleration of evil must be understood within the context of free will and freedom of choice. God allowed Adam and Eve to choose whether to obey him, and they yielded to the temptation to disobey.

Consequently they and the physical world were cursed by God, and the entire natural order was corrupted. Adam and Eve, too, were deeply affected in body, soul and spirit. They now experienced anxiety and fear for the first time. They now knew that they were weak and that they would die. And sin had taken up residence within them.

But what does it mean to say that sin resides in human nature? How does it operate there? We need to know how to deal with the sin that now masters our life, making beings who were originally created to worship and serve God serve a new master: Satan.

We also need to know how the Christian understanding of human nature differs from that in African Traditional Religion.

7

HUMAN NATURE

When we were children, there were many mysteries that baffled our imagination. How could witches be said to be drinking the blood and eating the flesh of people who still looked normal, except for their sickness? How could a newborn baby be said to be the reincarnation of an old man who died some time ago? We were told stories about elderly women returning to the village who met someone on the road who refused to answer their greetings. On reaching the village, the women would be told, "The person you met on the road has just died. You saw their ghost on its way to the city of the dead." Stories abounded about how the dead had been found living in distant lands, or had appeared to their relations in various circumstances.

As I have grown older, I have recognized that all these stories are not simply about miraculous phenomena. They also reflect the traditional African view of human nature and of the life force that animates it. These views have a profound influence on how African Christians deal with evil and sin.[38]

Traditional African View of Human Nature

Christians tend to think of people as consisting of a body, soul and spirit. By contrast, African Traditional Religion tends to identify the following four basic components of human nature:[39]

- *Breath* is a vivifying principle, a life force which links each individual with other life forces in the universe and is in vital relationship with them.

- *The destiny soul*, which is an emanation or spark of the Creator within the individual.
- *The ancestral guardian spirit* that is incarnate in the individual and links each individual with the life force of the clan, family or other human group.
- *The unique individual* created by God.

It is important for us to grasp the principle that in African thinking every human being is linked to other life forces, which we can call spirit beings or spirit powers.[40] This linkage is not merely a spiritual matter but manifests itself in the physical world. The human person is a conduit through which spirit powers operate, and these powers may choose to express themselves in ways that are evil, such as witchcraft and demonic activities. Thus Africans are deeply fearful of them. Even African Christians experience anxiety because they see themselves as linked to these spirit powers. That is why they need to hear the message that Paul proclaims in Colossians, when he says that "having disarmed the powers and authorities, he [Christ] made a public spectacle of them, triumphing over them by the cross" (Col 2:15). The cross of Christ breaks our bondage to the spirits.

Traditional Africans also conceive of human beings as a composite of assembled parts, rather than as a unity. Evil may not necessarily attack the whole person, but it can attack the most vulnerable parts. Body parts such as hair and body fluid can also be used as vehicles to attack someone. This belief, too, leads to living in perpetual fear of an attack by spirit powers that are manipulated by witchcraft, and a desire to find some way to shield one's body from such attacks. Parents, even Christian parents, will use charms or other spiritual powers to try to ward off spiritual attacks. They need to be taught that the cross of Christ offers protection against these attacks, too, so that they can be like those who "triumphed ... by the blood of the Lamb and by the word of their testimony" (Rev 12:11). We will look at this in more detail in the chapter in which we address anxiety and fear in regard to questions of evil, sin, fate, death and destiny.

It is traditionally believed that when someone dies, their physical body rots in the grave but their spiritual element lives on and joins the living dead, provided the deceased is given proper burial rites and is remembered by his or her descendants. If the burial rites and ceremonies are not properly performed, the spirit may become malevolent. This is the fate of witches, sorcerers, wicked people and those who died a violent or mysterious death.

The ancestral spirits play a significant role in the African understanding of human nature, even among African Christians who desire to maintain a spiritual bond with their living relatives and to be remembered after death.

Given this understanding of human nature, it is easy to understand why an individualistic approach to sin or spirituality has little impact in Africa. Ikenga-Metuh describes each human being in Africa as:

> a force in a universe of living forces, a member of the community of men and at the same time a unique individual endowed with a unique destiny which only he himself can realize ... Man is linked to the universe of forces by an ontological principle from inside man himself. Through his life-force ... he can influence and be influenced by other forces outside himself. This life-force can be strengthened, weakened and may die. Man is integrated into his family, clan and other social groups through another potent principle – ancestral life-force ... Through this, the life-force of the family flows in him. Man's individuality is assured by his personal destiny ... The supreme and ultimate goal of human life is the increase of his own life-force and the life-forces of the family and other groups to which he belongs. The greatest evil is the weakening or extinction of his life force.[41]

Traditional African thinking about human nature would also deny that all people are born sinners and are thus inherently evil. They see evil as something non-human, which can enter people. It can be inherited or passed on from one person to another. It can also be removed, if one knows the right rituals. This perspective conflicts with the Christian understanding that all human beings are corrupt and in need of redemption.

The African understanding of human nature informs how people in traditional Africa live and relate to the world around them. In fact, many African scholars believe that the traditional religion of Africa is anthropocentric, that is, it is focused not on God but on human life in the here and now. Laurenti Magesa even maintains that the promotion of life is at the heart of African life and morality.[42] The pursuit of material goods and physical safety tends to override the pursuit of right behaviour – except in so far as such behaviour will maintain good relations with the spirit powers. But putting effort into keeping these powers happy is a form of spiritual idolatry, rather than spirituality.

Biblical View of Human Nature

The Bible agrees with African Traditional Religion that every human being is both a physical and a non-physical being. The physical part is the body, while the spirit or soul is non-physical. At death the body rots in the grave, while the soul or spirit lives on.

Yet not all Christian theologians would accept what has been said above. Some claim to be monists, believing in the unity of the human being. They say that neither the body nor the soul or spirit can exist by itself and that every human being is a fusion of body and soul or spirit in one personality. Other theologians are dichotomists, who believe that human beings consist of two parts, namely a body and a spirit (or soul). Thus Wayne Grudem states, "Everything that the soul is said to do, the spirit is also said to do, and everything that the spirit is said to do, the soul is also said to do."[43] This statement is absolutely correct. However, it dwells only on the similarity of the roles and functions of the spirit and the soul, and does not theologically dissect the impact of the fall upon both. Still other theologians are trichotomists, who distinguish three distinct aspects of human nature, namely spirit, soul and body.

All these theologians claim to have scriptural basis for their views, and so it is important for us to examine the biblical data carefully and try to understand what the Bible is saying.

Spirit, Soul and Body

The Bible often uses the words "spirit", "soul" and "body", using all three together or separately. Thus Paul prays, "may your whole *spirit and soul and body* be kept blameless" (1 Thess 5:23). The writer of Hebrews speaks of God's word as "dividing *soul and spirit*" (Heb 4:12);

Mary sings, "My *soul* glorifies the Lord, and my *spirit* rejoices in God my Saviour" (Luke 1:46–47). The use of two different words in the same passage indicates not mindless repetition, but distinctions in the meaning of these words. Admittedly, the distinctions are subtle, which is why there is disagreement among scholars. So it will be good if we begin by defining these words carefully and seeing whether we can always substitute one for the other, or whether they occur in different contexts and have different meanings.

Once again, our starting point has to be the creation of human beings in Genesis 2:7: "The Lord God formed a man from the dust of the ground, and breathed into his nostrils the breath of life, and the man became a living being."

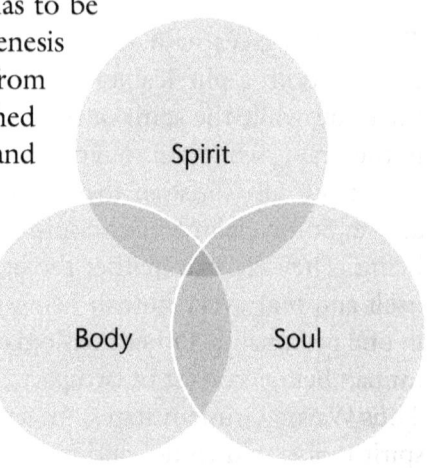

Human Nature (Gen 2:7)

The man's physical body was moulded from the dust. God reminds Adam of this after the fall, when he tells him, "dust you are and to dust you will return" (Gen 3:19). The human spirit was given when God breathed the breath of life into the man. This spirit animated the human body, so that the man became a *nepesh*, "a living being".

The Hebrew word translated "breathed" is *naphach*, which means, among other things, to puff, kindle, blow or breathe. We need to note that when God "breathes" into the man he is not turning the man into an emanation or an extension of himself. He is simply using his breath of power to create life where there was none, just as he used his word of power to create the world where there was nothing.

God's breath is like a spark that lights the fire that becomes the human spirit. Africans are thus right to speak of human beings as being like sparks. But the human spirit, the breath (*neshamah*) of life that the man received as a gift, is very different from the holy and transcendent Spirit of God. The breath of life is simply the breath of God's life power, which gives life. When Jesus says that "the Spirit gives life" (John 6:63), his point is that the Holy Spirit gives life to the human spirit. It did that at creation, and it can do it again to give us eternal life in Christ.

When God breathed into him, the man became a *nepesh*, a breathing creature, a living, self-conscious being, or as the KJV translates it, "a living soul". This passage thus distinguishes between the "breath of life", the principle of life that animates a body, and "becoming a living being," which refers to the totality of the man's existence. He becomes more than just a living being that breathes; he is a *nepesh* that thinks and does things. The spirit that animates the body is quite distinct from the inanimate moulded dust (the body) that became alive (a soul). This soul is distinct from the spirit that animates the body, just as the physical body that has been animated is distinct from the soul, which is a non-physical life principle.

God intended the human spirit, soul and body to operate in a trinitarian harmony, in which the spirit would rule over the soul and the body; the soul would take orders and directives from God through the spirit and command and direct the body; and the body would obey and execute the will of God. Together they would fulfil the sole purpose of our creation, which is to worship, serve and obey God.

But this harmony has been broken by the fall, and the roles of the spirit and the soul have become confused. Yet it is important to distinguish them if we are to come to a thorough understanding of the effect of sin on every part of human nature.[44]

Sin and the spirit

The primary function of the spirit as God gave it at creation was to enable human beings to commune with God. The spirit was supposed to direct both soul and body in worship and service of him. It is still the source of the God-consciousness that manifests itself in three main areas of our lives: our conscience, our intuition and our communion with God.

Conscience is the faculty of the spirit that spontaneously discerns what is right and what is wrong. Whenever we do wrong, our conscience accuses us – although we tend to respond by silencing it. Thus Paul can describe people who deliberately mislead believers as those "whose consciences have been seared as with a hot iron" (1 Tim 4:2) and speak of people whose "minds and consciences are corrupted" (Titus 1:15).

The writer of Hebrews talks about Christ's role as the one who can "cleanse our consciences from acts that lead to death" (Heb 9:14).

Conscience provides us with spiritual discernment that is imparted by the Spirit of God rather than by reason or science, which are out of tune with spiritual matters. Africans recognize this, and when people are faced with impossible situations, incurable sicknesses, unimaginable circumstances and calamities, they search for deeper truths in the spirit realm. Those who believe in African Traditional Religion call for diviners. Christians should learn from their attitude and seek to cultivate spiritual discernment and the wisdom revealed by the Spirit (1 Cor 2).

Intuition is the faculty of the spirit that senses non-human communication or knowledge. We come to know some things not by physical or intellectual means but because the Holy Spirit reveals them to our spirits. Scripture supports this idea, for God told Jeremiah, "Call to me and I will answer you and tell you great and unsearchable things you do not know" (Jer 33:3). Peter also asserts that "No prophecy of Scripture came about by the prophet's own interpretation. For prophecy never had its origin in the human will, but prophets, though human, spoke from God as they were carried along by the Holy Spirit" (2 Pet 1:20–21). God still speaks to us and he may do so without using any of our senses. However, because of the fall and our own sinfulness, we can hardly hear or sense the Holy Spirit in our lives. As the Bible says, "The person without the Spirit does not accept the things that come from the Spirit of God" (1 Cor 2:14). As believers, we need to practise prayer and meditation in order to cultivate the habit of sensing what the Holy Spirit is saying to us.

Westerners, with their faith in reason and science, find it particularly difficult to accept that there is a spiritual way of knowing, but traditional Africans are quite comfortable with this concept. Unfortunately, however, the spiritual idolatry in African Traditional Religion means that their spiritual dealings are not done directly with God but with surrogate spirit powers and spirit beings. We need to relearn how to listen to God himself.

Communion is the faculty of the spirit that worships God. We do not know God through our senses, our thoughts, imaginations or feelings. He can only be known through our spirit as the Holy Spirit imparts himself to us or communicates with us through our spirit. This reflects the truth that the primary function of the spirit in the beginning was to enable us to commune with God and to direct both soul and body in worship and service of God.

The fall deeply affected the human spirit. Instead of leading us in worship of God, it became averse to him, even hating him, and working against him. Instead of ruling in harmony over the soul and body, the spirit lost control of both of them, and even became subject to them. It is now ruled by spiritual surrogates and spirit powers that have usurped the place of God. There is much truth in the African traditional understanding of how different parts of the human body affect the total life of a human being.

Our confusion about the difference between the spirit and the soul is itself rooted in the fall, for the spirit now copies and imitates the soul, and the soul in turn copies and imitates the spirit. Both are corrupted, and both exhibit the characteristics of deception, duplicity, inconsistency and contradiction.

When the fallen spirit is subservient to the fallen soul and body, it becomes self-centred rather than God-centred. It no longer directs us to what is good but to what will satisfy our selfish desires and our sensuality. It is useless when it comes to directing us to God. It serves a new master.

But the spirit has not entirely forgotten its original role, and that is why we endure internal warfare, as the body, soul and spirit strive for mastery and form shifting alliances. No wonder we feel that our lives are full of crises, contradictions and inconsistencies. There is a great war going on within us, among and between the faculties of our fallen being. Scripture recognizes this and speaks of "sinful desires, which wage war against your soul" (1 Pet 2:11) and of "your desires that battle within you" (Jas 4:1). The only relief from this condition is to turn to Christ, who will renew, sanctify and transform our spirit so that it can serve God again. Then we will become true worshippers who can "worship the Father in the Spirit and in truth" (John 4:23).

Sin and the soul

The soul is the seat of human personality and self-consciousness. At creation the union between the spirit and body resulted in man becoming a *nepesh*, a soul. The soul blends the spirit and the body together to communicate and cooperate and is what makes us human. In fact, in

Hebrew the word "soul" is often used when speaking of the whole person (as is clear from the KJV translation of the genealogies in Genesis 46).

The activities of the soul are apparent in our volition (that is, our will or heart), our mind (that is, our intellect, thought and reason), and in our emotions (that is, our affections, desires and feelings).

Volition is the faculty of the soul that involves decision-making. It gives us the power to choose to do good or evil and the capacity to originate things or events.[45] It is at work when we say that we will or won't do something. Thus it plays a very important role in our lives, for it determines and governs our actions.[46]

In many places, the word translated as "will" or "desire" or "greed" in our Bibles is actually the word *nepesh*, which literally means "soul". We see this in Psalm 27:12, 41:2, and in Ezekiel 16:27. In other places, the soul is said to be what chooses a course of action (1 Chr 22:19; Job 7:15).

After the fall, sin attached itself to our wills and hearts like a virus. The result is that our desires are now always corrupted in some way. Our will and our heart are directed away from God and his holy things.

The *mind* is the faculty of the soul that is the centre of our thoughts, intellectual activities, knowledge, wisdom, reason, perception, speculation, understanding, discernment and imagination.[47] The psalmist talks of taking "counsel in my soul" (Ps 13:2, NKJV). He also speaks of the wonders of the human body as something that "my soul knows very well" (Ps 139:14, NKJV). The writer of Proverbs describes wisdom and discretion as bringing "life to your soul" (Prov 3:21–22, NKJV) and says that fearing the Lord will ensure that "knowledge is pleasant to your soul" (Prov

SPIRIT
Conscience
Intuition
Communion

BODY
Physical/
manual
labour

SOUL
Mental/
intellectual
labour
Volition
Emotion

Human Nature

2:10, NKJV). In the New Testament, the Apostle Paul instructs believers, "Do not conform to the pattern of this world, but be transformed by the renewing of your mind" (Rom 12:2). Our minds need renewal because they have been corrupted by sin. Our thoughts, intellect, knowledge, wisdom, reason and understanding are all infected with this virus. The result is that our attention is diverted from God and our minds focus only on what this world offers.

Emotion is the faculty of the soul that is the centre of our likes or dislikes. It affects whether we respond with hate or love, with desire or rejection. In this it works closely with the mind in shaping the way we think about something. In fact the activities of all the faculties of the soul are interrelated and intertwined. They never operate in isolation.

At creation, God intended this dominant human nature, the soul or self, to be under the authority of the spirit. But after the fall the soul took over power and now dominates both the spirit and body. It even seeks to take over from the spirit in regard to religion and spiritual matters by seeking to act like a priest or ruler.

In 1 Corinthians 2:14–3:4 the Apostle Paul makes a distinction between those who are "worldly", that is, those who are still led by the body and the soul, and those who are spiritual, who are dominated and controlled by the Holy Spirit. The Holy Spirit has imparted himself to them and they now live in newness of life, doing what is pleasing to God.

Sin and the body

Whenever a human being submits to a spiritual power, whether God or any other power, that power controls that person. Similarly, whenever a human being surrenders his or her body to sensuality and the works of the flesh, the body rules that person.

The body, which God formed for us from the dust of the earth, makes us aware of the world around us. It is "the focal point of our presence in the physical world and social world."[48] It is with our bodies that we experience the sensations of taste, touch, smell, sight and hearing. It is with our bodies that we relate to other people and to our environment. It is with our bodies that we show our love for God: "Love the Lord your God with all your heart and with all your soul, and with all your mind and with all your strength" (Mark 12:30). Our body is more than just dust; it is also the temple of God if his Spirit lives within us (1 Cor 3:16–17).

Unfortunately, the fall has adversely affected the body. It now seeks to overpower both the soul and the spirit and dominate them through its sinful desires, passions, sensuality, lust and greed. Instead of keeping our bodies holy and pure, as befits the temple of God, we take our bodies and use them to do all kinds of shameful things. These include many of the rituals, blood sacrifices, ceremonies and festivals that characterize African Traditional Religion. Thus the body too needs deliverance from sin. Paul exhorts the Colossians to "put to death … whatever belongs to your earthly nature" (Col 3:5).

Conclusion

Spiritual idolatry involves the giving of our spirit, soul and body to causes that are opposed to God. This is what all of us now do, for sin has infected every part of our human nature. Thus sin is not just something we do with our bodies, it involves everything in us. Our way of life is controlled by our thoughts, feelings, choices, bodily desires and social context – and all these faculties have been corrupted by sin so that we live in sin. God's creation of human beings with a spirit, soul and body has been deformed, defaced and disrupted by the fall. It is only by his grace and by the cross of Christ that we can return to a godly way of life that is ruled by the Spirit of God.

PART II:
THE TRINITY OF SIN

Part I of this book laid the theological groundwork for our thinking about sin in general. We looked at how it came into the world and how it affects all aspects of our human nature. Now it is time to look more specifically at the three pairs of root sins that constitute a trinity of sin.

Please do not be misled by this name. I am not implying that there is any similarity between these sins and the Holy Trinity of God the Father, God the Son and God the Holy Spirit. The term *trinity of sin* is simply a convenient way of reminding ourselves that the Bible shows that all our different types of sins can be categorized in terms of three pairs of root sins: self-centredness and pride, greed and lust, and anxiety and fear.[49] The sins in each pair are similar, inseparable and complimentary.

In Part II of the book, we will look closely at each of these pairs, examining how they first manifested themselves, their effect on human nature, and the many ways in which they manifest themselves today. Recognizing where a specific sin is rooted is key to diagnosing it and knowing what treatment is required to eradicate it.

The spade with which we will dig to expose these root sins will not be classical theology or philosophy or human traditions. No, our spade will be the Bible.

Three Pairs of Root Sins

9

SELF-CENTREDNESS AND PRIDE

[God] made two kinds of creatures to know Him, to wit, the angelic and the human. Pride shattered each of them
— Gregory the Great

The first pair of root sins that we will consider is self-centredness and pride. This pair manifests itself in sinful attitudes. A sinful attitude is derived mainly from counterfeit knowledge and wisdom. This was what the Tempter offered to Eve, and it was what changed Eve's attitude to God's command. My reason for choosing this pair as the starting point is that "pride is the beginning of sin, the first impulse and movement toward evil".[50] It was the lever that Satan used to pry open Eve's human heart so he could take residence there and corrupt her very self, and the selves of all her descendants.

> **SELF, WISDOM AND KNOWLEDGE**
>
> Self-centred knowledge arouses the selfishness and pride that are the root of all sinful attitudes
>
> Genesis 3:6

Defining Pride

In the Gyong language of Nigeria, pride is referred to as *gyong rikhe*, which literally means that someone has a "big head" or a "swollen head". Closely associated with it is the phrase *nnyoky rikhe*, which literally means a "raised head" or "arrogance". The words convey a vivid picture of people who are full of their own importance and strut around thinking that they are head and shoulders above all others. They assume a status to which they are not entitled.

But pride is not always bad. There are things that are legitimately great. We can celebrate the majesty of God (Isa 24:14) and our status as his people (Ps 47:4).[51] We can take pride in what God is doing in our lives. We can take pride in the good things others accomplish, or even in ourselves when our motives are pure and we are not out to exalt ourselves by putting others down. But pride becomes evil when it serves our self-interest or makes us assume that the rules that apply to others do not apply to us. That is why the Bible uses the same word to dismiss the pride of the arrogant and self-confident (Jer 48:29).

A related group of Hebrew words are often translated as "arrogance" or "presumption".[52] This is the type of self-importance that leads to rebellion and wilful disobedience. It was what led the Israelites to ignore God's explicit command and march into Canaan even after he had forbidden them to do so (Deut 1:43).

Yet another group of Hebrew words for pride centre on the idea of "lifting up"[53] and express the same lofty sense of self-importance as the "raised head" identified as a sign of pride in Gyong. This word is used of King Uzziah, of whom it is said that "when he was strong, his heart was lifted up to his destruction: for he transgressed against the Lord his God, and went into the temple of the Lord to burn incense upon the altar of incense" (2 Chr 26:16, KJV).

Looking at the words translated as "arrogance" or "pride" in the New Testament also gives us insight into what pride involves. For example, the word *hypselophroneo* is used when referring to those who put their trust in something other than God himself (Rom 11:20; 1 Tim 6:17). The words *physioo* (1 Cor 4:6, 18, 19; 5:2; 8:1; 13:4; Col 2:18) and *physiosis* (2 Cor 12:20) address the inner effect of pride in puffing us up – in other words, giving us a "big head" as the Gyong would say. *Authades* (Titus 1:7 and 2 Pet 2:10) is used to refer to people who are "self-willed", "stubborn" or "arrogant".[54]

Putting all these ideas about pride together, it is clear that what underlies it is the desire to be autonomous, that is, to be able to exist and make decisions apart from God. It leads people to treat God as irrelevant and to seek for knowledge and wisdom without any reference to his Holy Spirit. They become selfish and self-centred. Wisdom and knowledge, which are good in themselves, are transformed into arguments that set themselves up "against the knowledge of God (2 Cor 10:5).

The rejection of God is the greatest sin of pride. Knowledge and wisdom that transform themselves into pride breed rebellion, disobedience and transgression. They break all the boundaries that God sets for his creatures. Pride sets us against our Creator and Maker. Pride makes us unbreakable and obstinate. In our self-centredness, our Creator becomes our enemy.

The Sin of Pride in Satan

Pride is rightly called the "spirit of Satan" for the sin of pride was what led to Satan's fall from heaven: "Your heart became proud on account of your beauty, and you corrupted your wisdom because of your splendour" (Ezek 28:17). Isaiah puts it this way: "You said in your heart, 'I will ascend to the heavens; I will raise my throne above the stars of God; I will sit enthroned on the mount of assembly, on the utmost heights of Mount Zaphon. I will ascend above the tops of the clouds; I will make myself like the Most High'" (Isa 14:13–14).

The sin of pride is always characterized by lifting oneself up. It involves thinking more highly of oneself than of others. It is the desire to always be on top, above all others in status, power, authority, possessions or fame. A proud person is never satisfied, never content, never grateful, never thankful; they are always looking for more. They are full of greed, lust and covetousness.

Fundamentally, pride is a deep-seated rejection of the authority and sovereignty of God.

Pride and the Fall

Satan tempted Adam and Eve by appealing to the same spirit of self and pride that had caused his own downfall. He aroused it by playing on their desire for wisdom and knowledge.

It is not that there is anything wrong with a desire for wisdom. In fact, Proverbs commends the search for it, saying "Blessed are those who find wisdom, those who gain understanding (*Prov 3:13*). *But Satan tempted Eve to get wisdom by disobeying God's explicit* instruction. He promised her a wisdom that would lift her up to the same level as God, saying that "when you eat of it your eyes will be opened, and you will be like God, knowing good and evil" (Gen 3:5).

Eve failed to recognize that all three of the supposed "blessings" that would flow from disobedience were counterfeit. So she listened to Satan, looked at the fruit and saw that it was "desirable for gaining wisdom" (Gen 3:6). She deliberately chose to disobey God and ate it.

Satan did keep his promise – in his own way. It was true that their eyes "were opened" (Gen 3:7) – but what were they opened to? Sin-consciousness and self-consciousness. They realized they were naked and that they were sinners. They were no longer a perfect reflection of God, for the image of God in them had been shattered. They were no longer good, holy and perfect, living with God as their king, but had set themselves up as independent agents.

The self or soul recognized that there was a power vacuum and seized the throne in their lives. Thus they did indeed become "like God", for they were worshipped. But how pitiful is self-worship and self-glorification!

They did gain knowledge of good and evil, just as Satan had promised. But it was a knowledge very different from the wisdom God gives, which is "pure ... peace-loving, considerate, submissive, full of mercy and good fruit, impartial and sincere" (Jas 3:17). Such wisdom brings us closer to God. The wisdom Adam and Eve gained was a proud wisdom that hates rules, despises authority, and embarks on a selfish quest for autonomy. It is characterized by bitter envy and selfish ambition (Jas 3:16). It alienates us from God, and ultimately produces the kind of despair felt by the writer of Ecclesiastes when he described all human wisdom as "meaningless".

Adam and Eve's sin has affected all of their descendants. The result is that we can no longer naturally make an unselfish choice to do good; all our choices are now contaminated by pride and self-centredness. These evils have become second nature to us as we try to promote, protect and defend our selves at any cost. What began as a sin against God rapidly also became a sin against others.

Self and Sin

Self-centredness is closely related to pride. Pride sets the self against God, and the self feeds on its own pride, like a dog eating its own tail or its own vomit. Our pride is strengthened and inspired by our self-love. Wherever the sinful self is found, there also is pride. And wherever pride is found, there also is the self. They are bedfellows, and so I often speak of them in conjunction as self-pride.

But what is the "self" I have been talking about? The word for "self "in Gyong is *rikhe mi* which literally means "my head", but refers to one's total being, everything that makes a person an individual, including their spirit, soul and body. These days we are all affected by what is called in Gyong, *yimi rikhe*, literally "the love of one's head". In other words, we are now preoccupied or obsessed with our own selves. Every action is weighed in terms of what we will gain from it. Our motives are selfish rather than selfless. We have little concern for others. Even when we try to be unselfish, there is "a baffling irresistible force that subtly twists each of our acts and intentions into a glorification of self that turns the self in on itself, so that all it does is done for its own glory and security".[55]

Because the self is our centre and the source of our actions and intentions, when it is tainted, everything else about us is tainted. Our spirit no longer yearns for God but instead celebrates its own self-righteousness. Our soul is affected, and we become self-willed and stubborn. Our body serves its own interests by indulging in greed, lust and worldly pleasures.

Sin always causes broken relationships and alienation. It breaks the relationship between the self and God. It breaks the relationship between the self and other human beings. It breaks the harmony that once existed between us and creation. Instead of being good stewards of the world God made, we have exploited and destroyed it. Finally, it breaks the unity that should exist within the self, and causes the self to be divided against itself. Our spirit, soul and body no longer act in harmony, and we are left confused and divided. The ultimate result of these broken relationships is that we suffer both physical and spiritual death. How could it be otherwise when we have alienated ourselves from God, who is the source of life? How could it be otherwise when we have corrupted the world so that we now live with physical, social and spiritual chaos, crisis and conflict?

Just as the eye can never see itself, so it is difficult for us to see our own selves and recognize the sinfulness which has invaded us. It may help us to recognize it and deal with it more effectively if we look at how the Bible describes it in terms of two basic areas of our lives: namely the heart and the flesh.

Heart and sin

When the Bible speaks of the human heart, it is not referring to the physical organ that pumps blood. In fact, we would be wrong to spend time trying to decide on the exact location of the biblical "heart" in the human body. Far more important is the question of where sin is located – is it inside or outside the human being? Answering this question is the first step to deciding how to deal with the problem of sin.

The traditional African answer would be that sin is located outside the human being. It is something external, an environmental pollutant. It is acquired by contact with unholy things, and the cure is some form of ritual washing. You may be surprised to know that this view of sin is very similar to that of the Pharisees. They believed that contact with certain things or eating certain food would make someone unclean. Jesus completely rejected the view:

> Don't you see that nothing that enters a person from the outside can defile them? For it doesn't go into their heart but into their stomach, and then out of the body ... What comes out of a person is what defiles them. For it is from within, out of a person's heart, that evil thoughts come – sexual immorality, theft, murder, adultery, greed, malice, deceit, lewdness, envy, slander, arrogance and folly. All these evils come from inside and defile a person. (Mark 7:18–23)

Jesus refers to the heart as a storehouse of evil, saying: "An evil man brings evil things out of the evil stored up in his heart" (Luke 6:45). The Apostle James said the same thing when he pointed out that temptation does not come from God but from our own evil desires (Jas 1:13–15).

Or as John Owen says, "Temptations do not put anything into a man which is not there already."[56]

Sin is thus rooted in the heart, in our inner being. That is where it has set up its headquarters, and from there it exercises control over every part of us. John Owen liked to describe sin as a tyrant that has captured the human heart and made it an impregnable fortress from which to maintain its rebellion against God.

What else do we know about the human heart?

- *The heart is unsearchable.* "We do not even know the secret intrigues and schemes, twists and turns, actions and tendencies of our own hearts."[57] The only one who can know it is the Lord, who says, "I the Lord search the heart and examine the mind" (Jer 17:10).
- *The heart is sin's inaccessible refuge.* The heart is inaccessible, and is thus a place where sin's strength is secret and its presence is hidden. We may at times think we have eradicated sin in our lives, but it is only hiding in the impregnable human heart.[58]
- *The heart is the place where sin lies camouflaged.* Sin in our hearts is camouflaged by the darkness of our minds. Our wills and emotions have no desire to throw any light on our heart that would expose or challenge sin.
- *The heart is deceitful.* The prophet Jeremiah says, "The heart is deceitful above all things" (Jer 17:9). It is the battleground for the spirit and the soul as each seeks to deceive the other, and it becomes ever more deceitful and hypocritical.
- *The heart abounds in contradictions.* People are very contradictory: "they are both wise and yet foolish, open and yet reserved, facile and yet obstinate, non-vindictive and yet revengeful."[59] The reason for this confusion is that sin has upset this harmony that should exist between spirit, soul and body. "The will refuses to choose the good the mind discovers. The affections do not delight in what the will chooses. All rebel against one another."[60]

All the sins of self-centredness and pride reside in the human heart. But how do these sins express themselves in our lives? In answering this question, the Bible speaks of the role of the flesh.

Flesh and sin

While the heart provides a safe haven for sin, the flesh provides a workshop and market for it. It is the place where sin finds expression.[61]

In the Bible, the word "flesh" has many meanings.[62] It can be used to refer simply to the physical body, in which case it can mean either just the soft parts (muscles and internal organs) or the entire human body, including the bones and the blood.

At other times, it is used to refer to the whole of humanity, as when Isaiah says that "the glory of the Lord shall be revealed, and all flesh shall see it together (Isa 40:5, KJV).

In the New Testament, "flesh" is often used to refer to the combination of soul and body under the control of sin. Thus Jesus contrasts those who are born of the flesh and those who are born of the spirit (John 3:6). He specifies that no one who is born of the flesh can see the kingdom of God (John 3:3).

> No distinction is made as to whether the man is good, moral, clever, able and kind or whether he is bad, unholy, foolish, useless and cruel. Man is flesh. Whatever a man is born with pertains to the flesh and is within that realm ... Every man is controlled by that composite of soul and body called flesh, following both the sins of his body and the self of his soul.[63]

Everyone without Jesus Christ is dead in their trespasses and sins (Eph 2:1). The flesh cannot be reformed by any human means – whether education, culture or religion. Paul reaffirms this point when he says that "those who are in the realm of the flesh cannot please God" (Rom 8:8) and that "the flesh desires what is contrary to the Spirit, and the Spirit what is contrary to the flesh" (Gal 5:17). He is clearly using "flesh" as a metaphor for the power of sin in human life. He also gives a partial list of the work of the flesh that makes it clear that sin affects our spirit, soul and body: "The acts of the flesh are obvious: sexual immorality, impurity and debauchery; idolatry and witchcraft; hatred, discord, jealousy, fits of rage, selfish ambition, dissensions, factions and envy; drunkenness, orgies, and the like (Gal 5:19–21).

All sins produced by the spirit, soul and body are works of the flesh. The human body with all its senses is the channel through which all forms of sin are manifest, including those relating to self-centredness and pride.

Sins Related to Self-Centredness and Pride

We have defined pride as the sinful attitude of those who refuse to submit to God and think themselves superior to others. It is the attitude of those who put themselves and their desires first.

Such attitudes are sometimes easy to identify. For example, we all know of rulers and politicians who have drained their country's treasury and deposited huge sums in foreign banks. Such behaviour is rooted in the sins of pride and self-centredness. But it is not just the very powerful who are callous and self-centred. We also all know of local politicians, elders and even ordinary people who have diverted funds meant for others into their own pockets. Pride also shows itself in the ethnic or clan conflicts, wars, genocide and rebellions when one group tries to get ahead at the expense of another. In trying to eradicate these evils, we have focused on political and economic solutions, and have had little success. We have ignored the devastating influence of the sins of self and pride.

But attitudes are not always visible on the surface. We cannot just say, "do this, or don't do that, and you will avoid sinning". No, actions prompted by pride may even appear good and righteous. But not all that glitters is gold. What is important in God's eyes is the motive for which something was done.

When we are honest with ourselves, we will admit that very often our motives are suspect. We may do a good deed because of what we get out of it, in which case our motive is our own self-interest or pleasure, not God's glory or a desire to relieve human need.

Jesus exposed the hypocrisy of religious leaders who focused only on meeting the external requirements of the law. Like them, we find it easy to concentrate on outward conformity to certain rules. But Jesus insisted that true righteousness is determined not by deeds but by motives. What is important to God is the state of our heart. This emerges clearly in Jesus' teaching in the Sermon on the Mount in Matthew 5–7, where he addresses the foundations of human thought, acts, attitudes and behaviours and says things like this:

> For I tell you that unless your righteousness surpasses that of the Pharisees and the teachers of the law, you will certainly not enter the kingdom of heaven … You have heard that it was said, "You

shall not commit adultery." But I tell you that anyone who looks at a woman lustfully has already committed adultery with her in his heart ... Be careful not to practice your righteousness in front of others to be seen by them. If you do, you will have no reward from your Father in heaven. So when you give to the needy, do not announce it with trumpets, as the hypocrites do in the synagogues and on the streets, to be honoured by others. Truly I tell you, they have received their reward in full. But when you give to the needy, do not let your left hand know what your right hand is doing, so that your giving may be in secret. Then your Father, who sees what is done in secret, will reward you (Matt 5:20, 27; 6:1–4).

As we read these words, we should examine our own motives for giving, praying, fasting and the like.

This emphasis on attitudes and motives is where Christianity differs from both Traditional African Religion and Islam. Believers in these faiths are often very religious and are involved in all kinds of religious activities. But to them the performance of religious rites is more important than the motives for performing them. Christianity emphasizes both what we do and why we do it. It says that our acts count for nothing if they are done with the wrong motives. But it also says that it is not enough to have the right motives and attitudes if we fail to act. As James reminds us, "faith without deeds is dead" (Jas 2:26).

We do not have time to go into all the sins that flow from self-centredness and pride. Paul lists some of them when he speaks of the problems plaguing the Corinthian church: "discord, jealousy, fits of rage, selfish ambition, slander, gossip, arrogance and disorder" (2 Cor 12:20). Others are identified in the list at the end of this chapter. I suggest that you look at the list and think about the attitude and motives that lie behind each of these sins. Why would somebody accuse someone of something, knowing that the accusation was not true? Their motive must be self-interest or pride. Why would somebody be envious of someone else's property unless it offends their pride that someone has something that they do not have? Why would a politician kill his rival? Murder too is motivated by self-interest or pride.

As we can see, our human self-centredness and pride leads to physical, social and spiritual chaos, crises and conflict in human society.

Dealing with the Sins of Self-Centredness and Pride

When Satan tempted Adam and Eve and they accepted his offer of autonomy from God, he infected the whole world with his poisonous spirit of pride. Today, rulers and subjects, rich and poor, the knowledgeable and the ignorant, the wise and the foolish, the high and the low, all are dominated by this spirit of pride.

So right in the garden of Eden, after the fall, God instituted warfare against it. He announced that the spirit of pride would be defeated on the cross by Jesus Christ. We will look at what this means in more detail in a later chapter. But for the moment, it is enough to point out that what has been said should make it abundantly clear that the sins rooted in pride and self-centredness are subtle and can hide deep within our hearts. We may not even be aware of the motives that are leading us to act in a certain way until we stop and examine our hearts. Even for that we need the help of God, for it is very easy to offer superficial rationalizations that obscure the deeper roots of our actions. We need to pray like the psalmist: "Search me, O God, and know my heart" (Ps 139:23).

The deceitfulness of the heart also means that we cannot deal with sins of self-centredness and pride by making a general or blanket confession of sin. Nor can we deal with them by simply performing some religious activity. No – we need to peer deep within ourselves, and identify the specific sins that are blooming from these roots. We must repent and confess our lying, deceit, ridicule, slander, or whatever else our love of self has led us into. Then we must claim God's forgiveness through the blood of Christ.

Summary

Pride is born of an abnormal relationship between the self and wisdom or knowledge. After the fall, the Spirit of God left us, and left behind a spiritual vacuum, darkness and uncertainty that can never be filled by human wisdom or knowledge. But human pride attempts to fill it. It offers a counterfeit to true spirituality and true knowledge of God. This counterfeit spirituality can only be dealt with through the cross of Christ by crucifying the self with Jesus Christ on the cross.

Words Associated with the Sins of Self-Centredness and Pride*

accusation	doubt	rebellion
ambition	duplicity	reviling
arrogance	envy	prejudice
assassination	faultfinding	revenge
assault	flattery	revolt
vengeance	favouritism	ridicule
betrayal	rage and fury	selfishness
bitterness	gossip	self-interest
blasphemy	grumbling	self-righteousness
boasting	haughtiness	self-confidence
conceit	hatred	self-indulgence
conspiracy	humiliating	self-seeking
contempt	hypocrisy	slander
criticism	inciting	stubbornness
deception	indifference	pretence
denial	insults	pride
derision	killing	tempting
despising	lying	treachery
discrimination	malice	unbelief
dislike	mockery	unfaithfulness
disobedience	murder	refusing to forgive
disregard	partiality	unfriendliness

* *Warning*: Do not simply seek to identify these sins in others – use this list to examine your own heart.

9

GREED AND LUST

As human beings, we have basic needs that flow from the way God created us. We need food, shelter and clothing. We need to reproduce to maintain the human race and fulfil God's command to be fruitful and multiply. But with the fall, these natural needs were distorted as sin destroyed our modesty and moderation in relation to the basic necessities of human life. Natural enjoyment of the food God provided was replaced with gluttony and drunkenness. Some ate too much; others too little. Our natural desire for sexual intercourse was warped and turned to pornography and perversion. In short, our desire for the pleasures God gave us was warped. So was our imagination, and these days it joins with our corrupted bodies to lead us astray.

> **PLEASURE, THE EYES AND THE MIND**
>
> Pleasure arouses the desires that lead to all the sins of lust. Lust is the root of all sinful desires of the soul.
>
> Genesis 3:6

Defining Greed and Lust

While self-centredness and pride are associated with the desire for wisdom and knowledge, greed and lust originate in our desire for possessions and pleasure. Greed leads us to gratify the sinful desires of our bodies, and lust the sinful pleasures of the heart (mind). When our sinful flesh and sinful heart combine, they produce the sinful works of the flesh.

There was a twentieth-century saying, "Greed is good". That saying is wrong. Greed is completely wrong in every way. It has no element of goodness in it. The Hausa are right to say *kwadayi mabudin wahala* [greed is the source of all evil]. It is indeed at the root of all kinds of sins. Paul makes a similar point when he says that "the love of money is a root of all kinds of evil" (1 Tim 6:9).

Greed can be defined as an "insatiable desire for food, money, power, or material possessions".[64] Note the word "insatiable". It means that this desire is never satisfied. It thinks it will be satisfied by having the thing desired, but even when the thing is obtained, greed wants still more of it. Alternatively, greed leads us to be disappointed when our desires are realized, so that we merely shift the focus of our greed to something else. The quest to satisfy greed is doomed to futility. Its cravings are like opened graves or bottomless pits.

Lust is equally insatiable. But where greed usually involves the body's desire to eat or drink or touch something, lust is more in the mind. It is the passionate desire for pleasure. It involves far more than just the sexual desires we often associate with lust, and includes all sinful desires. "The lust of the eyes" is an excessive desire for things that please our eyes, and "the lust of the flesh" is a passionate desire to have power, money, possessions, or any other sensual gratification. Sinful sights, imaginations, thoughts and feelings feed and inflame our lusts.

Greed, Lust and the Fall

Eve was tempted by the suggestion that she could be her own source of wisdom, without any need for God. The Tempter persuaded her to look at the fruit of the forbidden tree with new eyes. She saw that it was attractive and desirable; "good for food and pleasing to the eye and also desirable for gaining wisdom". What she saw was true. The fruit had all these qualities, and there was nothing wrong with recognizing this. But she did not balance this recognition with a reminder that God had forbidden her to eat this fruit. Instead, she reached out, "took some and ate it" (Gen 3:6).

We could contrast this with Jesus' reaction when Satan tempted him with food in the wilderness. He was hungry after a long fast, and undoubtedly bread would be "good for food and pleasing to the eye". But he was able to reject that temptation, saying "Man shall not live on bread alone, but on every word that comes from the mouth of God" (Matt 4:4).

Temptation offers only possibility, not reality. It is when we give in to temptation that evil becomes real. Appropriating evil leads to conceiving and birthing sin. Once sin is birthed, we are no longer dominated by the Spirit of God but by spiritual evil. Eve's sin gave Satan and evil power over all her descendants.

Greed

We need food to survive, and the desire for it is good and natural. But Eve's disobedience marked a change from eating because we need to eat in order to stay alive to eating simply because we want to do so, and becoming obsessed with food. Our desire for food and our other bodily desires are no longer subordinate to our spirit but control our spirit. The God-appointed roles of mind and body have been reversed. This is a disastrous state to be in, for our appetites are insatiable. The departure of the Spirit of God has left a void that greed cannot fill.

> **BODY AND FOOD**
>
> Food arouses the desires that lead to all the sins of greed.
> Greed is the root of all sinful desires of the flesh.
>
> Genesis 3:6

Lust

Eve allowed her eye to linger on the forbidden fruit. She allowed her imagination to play with the idea of the pleasure to be gained by eating it. Here is the root of all the sinful desires that tempt us by teasing our imagination with pleasures that they claim will satisfy the needs of our eyes, mind and soul.

With the fall, the normal use of our eyes, mind, senses and soul was perverted. The normal and good pleasures of seeing, hearing, feeling, touching, imagining, sensing and thinking grew grotesquely out of proportion and we developed an insatiable desire for sinful pleasures. Our mind, will and thought were all affected, and there was no longer a harmonious relationship between our senses and the pleasures of God's created world.

Lust, too, offers a form of spirituality that seeks to fill the void left by the absence of the Spirit of God.

Self-centredness and Pride and Greed and Lust

Self-centredness is closely associated with greed, for it is the self that has the insatiable appetites that fuel greed. It is the self that cannot be satisfied without God, and yet refuses to turn to him. Instead, it seeks false satisfaction by encouraging the body to indulge in sinful excess.

Pride, on the other hand, works more on the soul and spirit. Pride is drawn to status, fame, honour, pomp and power, and it corrupts our thoughts and imagination by filling them with images of what we could enjoy and persuading our minds that we deserve them. In encouraging us to dwell on these images, it feeds our lust for the pleasures of the eyes and mind and soul.

In short, greed preoccupies itself with acquiring things that feed the body and the works of the flesh, while lust preoccupies itself with acquiring things that feed the soul and the works of the flesh. Both nourish our self-centredness and pride.

Sins Related to Greed and Lust

> The leech has two daughters, "Give! Give!" they cry.
> There are three things that are never satisfied, four that never say, "Enough!": the grave, the barren womb, land, which is never satisfied with water, and fire, which never says, "Enough!" (Prov 30:15–16)

Greed and lust are like that – they never say, "Enough!" They are like the wily African bird that skips a few yards away at a time, gradually luring the one hunting it into the wilderness until he becomes weary and lost. In the same way, greed and lust lure those seeking sinful pleasure into the wilderness of gluttony, drunkenness, passions, sensuality and perversion.

Greed undermines the just distribution of resources within societies and nations. Some people accumulate vast riches while condemning others to poverty by underpaying them, overcharging them, or destroying the natural environment on which they depend for food and water. Lust destroys families, marriages and relationships. It leads to broken treaties and agreements that unleash quarrels, feuds and wars. Together these root sins have unleashed intolerable social, economic and political suffering through the ages.

The way to identify sins of self-centredness and pride is to examine people's motives. Are they seeking glory for themselves? The way to identify sins rooted in greed and lust is to see whether people are seeking to gratify sinful desires. Sins rooted in a desire to gratify the body and flesh are sins of greed. They reflect an insatiable desire for food, money, power, possessions or sensuality. Sins that seek to gratify the soul and mind are sins of lust. They indulge sensual appetites. All of them seek to provide pleasure, happiness, enjoyment, delight, indulgence and satisfaction in sinful ways.

At the end of the chapter there is a random list of some of the sins sparked by greed and lust. You may be able to identify more.

Dealing with the Sins of Greed and Lust

At first glance it would appear that the answer to greed and lust is to get the thing desired. But that is not the case. As soon as the object is achieved, the goalposts are shifted. The reason is that we will never find the real object of our desire in anything less than God. All the other things we focus our desires on are only empty shells, like those we pick up on a beach and then throw down as something else captures our attention. We have an insatiable appetite for more.

Behind both greed and lust, there is only emptiness, a void. The Teacher who wrote Ecclesiastes understood this, for he had joined in the search for wisdom, riches and pleasure "under the sun", that is, on earth, without regard to God. He lamented that everything done under the sun is meaningless (or "vanity" in the KJV). Without God, everything is meaningless. Without him, we live in a spiritual desert and can never find enough of the food and water we crave.

We do make sporadic attempts to address the problems caused by our greed and lust. But none of our solutions work, as Jesus reminds us in his parable:

> When an impure spirit comes out of a person, it goes through arid places seeking rest and does not find it. Then it says, "I will return to the house I left." When it arrives, it finds the house swept clean and put in order. Then it goes and takes seven other spirits more wicked than itself, and they go in and live there. And the final condition of that person is worse than the first. (Luke 11:24–26)

When God is not present, Satan, evil and sin rush in to take his place. They dominate us and inflame our sinful desires. We cannot cleanse ourselves of their influence or repair the damage they have done. But this is what Jesus Christ can do as he repairs, renews and transforms us through the ministry of the Holy Spirit and the word, as we will see in a later chapter.

Words Associated with the Sins of Greed and Lust*

accumulation	coveting	impoverishing
adultery	craving	indulgence
alluring	dishonesty	injustice
amassing	drunkenness	intoxication
appetite	emptiness	jealousy
avarice	enticing	lasciviousness
bestiality	envy	lewdness
breach of trust	evil desire	looting
bribery	evil passion	luring
caressing	extortion	orgies
carousing	filthiness	perversion
cheating	fornication	promiscuity
clamouring	fraud	prostitution
concealing	gluttony	seduction
corruption	homosexuality	sensuality
cover-ups	immorality	stealing

* *Warning*: Do not simply seek to identify these sins in others – use this list to examine your own heart.

10

ANXIETY AND FEAR

Since the fall, we have had to defend ourselves against an environment that has become threatening. Not only do we face physical dangers from things like thorns and the scorching sun, but we are also threatened by other people, both physically and emotionally. Consequently, fear and anxiety have become necessary to preserve our lives. You would be foolish to walk down a path knowing that a pride of lions was resting next to it. You would be foolish not to be anxious enough to take water with you if your route led through a desert. The fears that lead us to take reasonable precautions are not sinful. But anxiety and fear become sinful when they drive us away from God, rather than towards him.

> **NAKEDNESS, SHAME AND OUR SINFUL NATURE**
>
> Nakedness is the awareness of sin and shame that leads to all the sins of anxiety.
>
> Genesis 3:7–8

Anxiety, Fear and the Fall

The Tempter promised Eve that if she ate the fruit she would "not certainly die … For God knows that when you eat from it your eyes will be opened, and you will be like God, knowing good and evil" (Gen 3:4). He dangled these promises in front of her, but did not tell her of the other consequences of disobedience to God. Adam and Eve not only gained knowledge, they also had their first encounter with anxiety and fear as they "realized they were naked" (Gen 3:7a).

They had thought they would see themselves as beings like God; instead, they became acutely aware of their sinful humanity. The nakedness that shamed them was not so much awareness that their bodies were not covered but rather awareness that they were no longer covered in God's glory. There was no joy in this transformation. They detested it. But they did not weep and turn to God. Instead, driven by sinful anxiety, they tried to remedy the situation for themselves and "sewed fig leaves together and made coverings for themselves" (Gen 3:7b). This was not an innocent act. It was the result of sin and was intended to cover up sin. It was a hopelessly inadequate remedy, as God's later action in providing them with garments of skin will show (Gen 3:21).

When we feel shame, it is because we realize that we, too, are fallen. Our shame is often followed by anxiety. What will we do about our situation? Too often, we choose to respond to this anxiety in ways that are sinful, rather than turning to God for his solution.

When Adam and Eve "heard the sound of the Lord God as he was walking in the garden ... they hid from the Lord God" (Gen 3:8). Previously, they were righteous and had no need to hide from God. But now they have broken God's command and are eager to avoid meeting him.

When God questions him, Adam blames his behaviour on his nakedness, but God sees through this excuse: "Who told you that you were naked? Have you eaten from the tree that I commanded you not to eat from?" (Gen 3:11). Nakedness was only a symptom. The real reason that he was hiding from God was because he had been disobedient to God's command. This alone is enough to rouse fear. Not only was he anxious about what to do about his newly sinful nature, but he was also afraid of what God would do to him because of his disobedience. He was anxious, ashamed, guilty and fearful.

He had good reason to be fearful. Standing before God, Adam and Eve heard him pronounce judgement on them and on all the earth for what they had done (Gen 3:11–19; 22–24). The Tempter had promised that Adam and Eve would not die if they ate the fruit of the tree. But when God spoke, he announced that Adam would "return to the ground, since from it you were taken; for dust you are and to dust you will return." Death had come into the world!

Defining Anxiety and Fear

In my Gyong language, the word translated "anxiety" is *shoukmen*, which literally means "a troubled mind" or "the rising of the mind". The word for worry is *thezamen*, which literally means "a spoilt or marred mind" or "a corrupted mind". A mind that is troubled, marred or corrupted cannot make good decisions.

The Hebrew word equivalent to "anxiety" in English also has negative connotations. We are told that "anxiety weighs down the heart" (Prov 12:25). Anyone who has endured living with a troubled or uneasy mind is well aware of this. When we are anxious, we are fearful about some situation and experience frustration and helplessness. Sometimes our anxiety is legitimate when it springs from our concern for others. A father may be anxious about his children's future, or a husband may worry about his wife's health. But we must be careful that the "worries of this life" do not preoccupy us to such an extent that God's word fails to bear fruit in our lives (Matt 13:22).

Some of our anxiety is simply because we fear that our hidden sins will be brought into the open. We are ashamed of what we are and of what we have done, and feel awkward, troubled and uneasy.

In Gyong, the word for "fear" is *gyou thyee* or *shangza*, which conveys the idea of the whole body trembling or shaking. Fear is an emotion that robs one of confidence in oneself or in someone else. It weakens our capacity to act. It causes us to flee, just as Adam and Eve did in the garden.[65] The basic cause of this fear is the awareness that one is vulnerable, whether to attack by another or to impending judgement.

Fear is not a bad thing when it takes the form of "the fear of the Lord", which the Teacher describes as "the beginning of knowledge" (Prov 1:7). We are right to recognize that we are powerless before God, and to reverence him and hold him in awe. He is the ultimate reality and the supreme Lord of the universe. We should not have this kind of fear for anything else. That is why there can be no other gods beside him (Exod 20:3; Deut 6:13).

Fear also comes when we anticipate something unpleasant happening to us. Thus when God called Moses and told him to go back to Egypt, Moses' fear led him to raise many objections (Exod 3 and 4). He failed to recognize God's command of events and human destiny.

Anxiety and fear become sins when they lead us to ignore God and try to save ourselves without God. A sinful anxiety drives us away from God to seeking our own solutions and salvation. A sinful fear drives us away from worshipping God to finding our own gods and worshipping them instead of our Creator and Maker.

Self-Centredness and Pride, Greed and Lust and Anxiety and Fear

The sin of pride led to rebellion against God. So God withdrew, and when he did so he took with him the covering of his glory, leaving human beings naked, empty, without communion and fellowship and without law and order. In response, we turned to greed and lust to gratify and satisfy ourselves. But we could not find happiness. All that we got was more misery, emptiness and meaninglessness. We also found ourselves ashamed of our sinful condition and guilty because of our disobedience and sin. Knowing that we deserve God's judgement and punishment, we feel weak, insecure and vulnerable. We no longer enjoy God's protection and cannot rely on God's sovereignty. We have no hiding place, no refuge, no shelter, no fortress.

The vacuum left by God's departure was not left empty for long. The human spirit was now open to all kinds of spiritual forces which embarked on a spiritual war to dominate us either by using the desire for pleasure to distract us from God or by increasing our fear of evil spirits so that we feared and obeyed them, rather than our Creator God.

Sins Related to Anxiety and Fear

The criterion for identifying sins related to self-centredness and pride is a sinful attitude and sinful motivation. The criterion for identifying sins related to greed and lust is that they pander to sinful desires. The criterion for identifying sins related to anxiety and fear is that they are sinful responses to recognition of our sinful nature and of sins we have committed.

The image of God in us has been disfigured and corrupted by sin. Yet many people live as if this has not happened. Some cling to a belief in progress and optimistically insist that people are getting better and better with the passing ages. Others, who are aware that something is wrong with us, seek to address the problem by turning to self-made gods and saviours. What they are doing is looking for their own "fig leafs" to cover the sinfulness in their natures. But all human remedies are merely temporary, and leave us burdened with a sense of anxiety. We are still haunted by our awareness of our sinful nature.

> **TRANSGRESSION, GUILT AND FEAR**
>
> Breaking God's law arouses guilt that leads to all the sins of fear.
>
> Genesis 3:7–8

Many people deny their own sinfulness. They think that on balance they lead moral lives and are kind to other people. They have failed to recognize that their sinful nature warps what they do, so that they are committing sins and rebelling against God even if they deny it. Yet while they deny that they have sinned, they also live in fear of having their sin exposed. They have to keep their eyes tight shut to avoid seeing it.

When we get so far as to recognize that we have done wrong, we often choose to run away and hide from God. We do not go directly to him, but instead seek our own intermediaries or mediators, of the type that are so plentiful in African Traditional Religion. We hope that performing some ritual will bring us forgiveness. And to avoid exposing our own nakedness and sin, we use our knowledge of good and evil as ammunition to raise ourselves up and pull others down. Sin is at the root of our anxiety, fear and defensiveness. We devote our time and resources to defending not what is necessary or normal in life, but our comforts, pleasures, passions, greed and lusts.

Our sins and our sinful nature are not the only issues that generate anxiety and fear. So does our awareness that we are creatures. We are not the lords of the universe; rather, we are weak and our lives and circumstances are vulnerable to forces beyond our control.

> Men are also deeply troubled by anxious fears arising from their weakness as creatures. The feeling of dependence and contingency, of being subject to uncontrollable forces, form the content of one of these anxieties. The experience of temporality and mortality, of an approaching dateline to one's powers and life, forms the frightening content of the other.[66]

What use is human intelligence if we can be wiped out by wars, genocide or epidemics? What purpose is there in work if all the proceeds of our labour are wiped out during some political, economic, or natural disaster? Can science really save us from diseases like cancer, HIV/AIDS and diabetes? Can it roll back the effect of the advancing years on our body? Rather than relying on God's sovereignty, we desperately try to acquire life force and spiritual power to beat back the evils and insecurity of the world. We have no time or energy to spend on the issues of justice, peace, righteousness and acts of kindness, mercy and love.

We can identify sins of anxiety and fear by observing the presence of emotions and actions that reflect exposure of sin's nakedness, shame or guilt, or human limitations and weaknesses. When people experience such states of mind, their reactions are based on their inner nature. How do those who do not believe in God react to death? Their reaction will be different from that of strong believers in God. Believers will have faith, trust and confidence in God, while others will be filled with anxiety and fear.

Below is a random list of words related to the conditions or states that generate anxiety and fear. It does not specifically include sinful actions. After all, what action does one take when facing death or humiliation or misery or despair? One person may choose to stop believing in God since he failed to prevent the death of a loved one. Someone else may kill a person who humiliated him in public. Another may commit suicide. Our feelings of fear and anxiety can find expression in myriad ways.

Dealing with the Sins of Anxiety and Fear

Just as the antidote for pride is humility, so the antidote for fear is the realization that God is sovereign. He is the only one whom we should fear, and once we fear him, we need fear nothing else. As the psalmist said, "When I am afraid, I put my trust in you. In God, whose word I praise – in God I trust and am not afraid. What can mere mortals do to me?" (Ps 56:3–4). Our fears should drive us to God and not away from him.

In subsequent chapters, we will deal with Jesus' teachings on anxiety and worry and the cares of this life, as well as with the ultimate cure for our fallen natures, our sins, and the fear they generate. This cure is found in the cross of Christ.

*Words Associated with the Sins of Anxiety and Fear**

fear	groaning	shame
agony	helplessness	sickness
anguish	hopelessness	madness
anxiety	horror	misery
guilt	humiliation	misfortune
brokenness	hurting	moaning
despair	lamentation	penalty
discouragement	misery	perplexity
disgrace	mourning	shuddering
dishonour	pain	terror
displeasure	panic	timidity
distress	perplexity	trembling
dread	poverty	turmoil
embarrassment	unhappiness	worry
frustration	unrest	
grief	insecurity	

* *Warning*: Do not simply seek to identify these sins in others – use this list to examine your own heart.

PART III: GOD'S SOLUTION TO THE PROBLEM OF SIN

By this stage, you should have realized four important points about our own condition:

- We all have a sinful nature which we inherited from Adam and Eve's sin.
- Our sinful nature makes it impossible for us to have a good relationship with God.
- All our actions are also tainted by sin.
- We are all vulnerable to temptation.

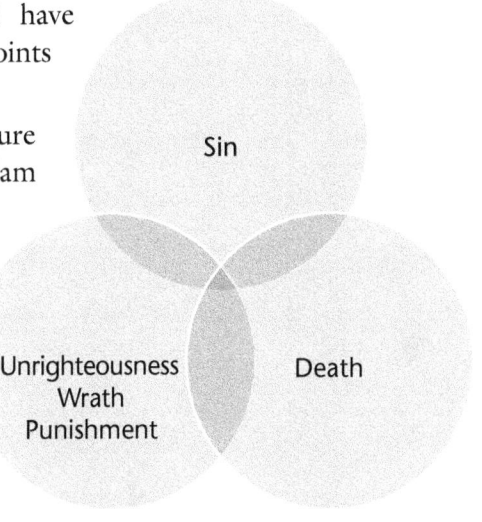

Our Heritage in Adam

The spirit powers, Satan, evil, sin and the world affect us all, even those of us who are believers in Jesus Christ. John Owen was clear about this when he stated: "Sin sometimes appears to topple strong believers overnight. But sin often causes a gradual decline in zeal and holiness in believers' obedience to – and communion with – God."[67] We see this clearly in the Bible too. The letters to the seven churches in Revelation 2 and 3 reveal their gradual moral decline. Giants of faith such as Noah, Lot, David, Solomon and Hezekiah all fell into sin. In our own day, we have seen the church rocked by scandals involving televangelists, paedophiles and homosexuality.

Given our vulnerability to sin, what hope do we have? We cannot use willpower to handle our own sin because our will itself is sinful and self-centred: "a will cannot will to change itself; a self that is diseased cannot provide its own health."[68] Rather we need God's solution, which he provided in the redemptive work of Jesus Christ on the cross and in the ministry of the Holy Spirit in regeneration and sanctification.

In the chapters that follow, we will see how God addresses our sin and how we can have victory over root sins by applying the power of the cross of Christ.

11

REDEMPTION IN JESUS CHRIST

I grew up in the early 1950s when Christianity was just beginning to make inroads into our part of Africa. African Traditional Religion was still a powerful force with its blood sacrifices, rituals, ceremonies, festivals, sacred days, months and years. I could discuss these, but I prefer to be guided by two African sayings. The first is ancient: "When we are discussing men of valour, don't bring grasshoppers into the conversation." The second is modern: "After eating pounded yams, Western dessert is an anticlimax." The ways of African Traditional Religion were not all wrong, but they find their eternal fulfilment in the once and for all sacrifice of our Lord Jesus Christ on the cross. There is no need to return to the past, for

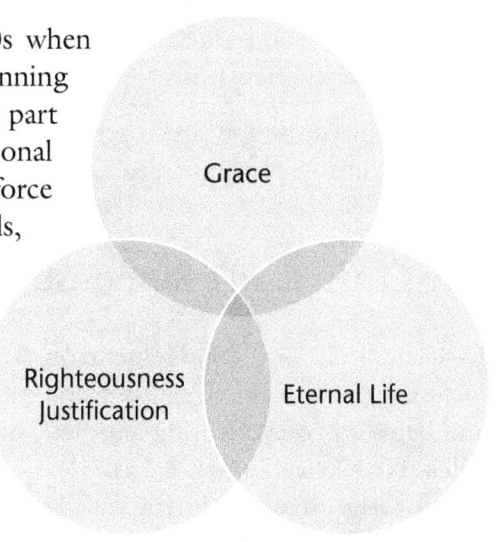

Believer's Heritage in Jesus Christ

> where there are prophecies, they will cease; where there are tongues, they will be stilled; where there is knowledge, it will pass away. For we know in part and we prophesy in part, but when completeness comes, what is in part disappears. (1 Cor 13:8–10)

Talk about the intermediaries or mediators in African Traditional Religion is like chatter before a serious talk begins.

> In the past God spoke to our forefathers through the prophets at many times and in various ways, but in these last days he has spoken to us by his Son, whom he appointed heir of all things, and through whom he made the universe. The Son is the radiance of God's glory and the exact representation of his being, sustaining all things by his powerful word. After he had provided purification for sins, he sat down at the right hand of the Majesty in heaven. So he became as much superior to the angels as the name he has inherited is superior to theirs. (Heb 1:2–4)

When Jesus Christ appeared on the scene, he silenced all boastful suitors and competitors for humanity's allegiance.

The Cross: God's Response to the Fall

In Genesis 3, God's judgement on Satan hidden within the serpent included the words, "I will put enmity between you and the woman, and between your offspring and hers; he will crush your head, and you will strike his heel" (Gen 3:15).

All those involved in the fall deserved to die. The serpent was a murderer for it brought death into the world, and God's decree is that, "Whoever sheds human blood, by humans shall their blood be shed, for in the image of God has God made mankind" (Gen 9:6). Adam and Eve deserved to die, for "the one who sins is the one who will die" (Ezek 18:20). But there was a difference. The serpent would be crushed under a curse. Eve, however, could be redeemed by a blood sacrifice, prefigured in the law of Moses and fulfilled in Jesus' death on the cross.

God in his infinite wisdom used the same tools used for the temptation and fall to accomplish his eternal plan of salvation and redemption. A tree had been the physical factor in the temptation, and a tree – the cross – would be a key factor in redemption.

The serpent was the agent Satan used in the temptation in the garden. Many years later, the Israelites would be attacked by venomous serpents in the wilderness because of their sins. Moses made a bronze serpent and set it up on a pole (or tree), and those who looked at it were saved. Jesus used this incident as an example when he said that "Just as Moses lifted up the snake in the wilderness so the Son of Man must be lifted up, that everyone who believes may have eternal life in him" (John 3:13).

According to the Old Testament, being hanged on a tree or a pole was a curse (Gal 3:13; Deut 21:23). Jesus took the curse that was placed on Eve on himself, and at the same time he crushed Satan, the serpent, fulfilling the curse in Genesis 3:15. As he hung there, Satan was bruising his heel. It was Satan who had entered Judas (John 13:27) and "wicked men" nailed Jesus to the cross (Acts 2:23). Yet at the same time, Jesus was crushing Satan's head, conquering the power of Satan, the power of sin, the power of death and the power of the world.

Eve was the first human being to listen to Satan, as Paul reminds us when he says that "it was the woman who was deceived and became a sinner" (1 Tim 2:14). Yet despite this, God incorporated her into his eternal plan of salvation, and promised that it would be her offspring that would eventually crush Satan (Gen 3:15). The rest of the Bible traces the history of that group of her descendants through whom this offspring would be born. We watch as God chooses Abraham, then Isaac (rejecting Ishmael), then Jacob (rejecting Esau), then Judah (rejecting his eleven brothers), then David and his descendants, and ultimately Mary, through whom Jesus Christ would come into the world.

Satan was "incarnated" in the serpent in that he took on the form of a serpent in order to deceive Eve. There was no such deception when the Word of God became flesh and was born the Son of God (John 1:14). The angel Gabriel spoke to Mary, saying

> Do not be afraid Mary; you have found favour with God. You will conceive and give birth to a son, and you are to call him Jesus. He will be great and will be called the Son of the Most High. The Lord God will give him the throne of his father David, and he will reign over the house of Jacob forever; his kingdom will never end. (Luke 1:31–33)

In Matthew's Gospel, we are told that the name "Jesus" means Saviour, "because he will save his people from their sins". The child is also called Immanuel, "which means 'God with us'" (Matt 2:21, 23).

In eating the fruit, Eve has been moved by the desire to gain wisdom (Gen 3:6). But rather than gaining life and wisdom, she learned about death and folly. Jesus, her offspring, had to replace that death and foolishness with life and wisdom. He knew that the way to wisdom lay through taking on her folly, and so he accepted the foolishness of the cross. Paul was alluding to this when he said that

> the message of the cross is foolishness to those who are perishing, but to us who are being saved it is the power of God ... God was pleased through the foolishness of what was preached to save those who believe ... we preach Christ crucified: a stumbling block to Jews and foolishness to Gentiles, but to those whom God has called, both Jews and Greeks, Christ the power of God and the wisdom of God. (1 Cor 1:18, 21–24)

The woman and the serpent were cursed and had to die for their sins. Jesus died to remove the sin, curse and death. By his resurrection he demonstrated that he had done this. Satan's head was crushed, his power was broken, and he would be brought to judgement (Rev 19–20).

Adam and the Second Adam

Adam's descendants have been tormented not only by the sinful nature we have inherited from him but also by the spirit powers of Satan, "the authorities ... the powers of this dark world and ... the spiritual forces of evil in the heavenly realms" (Eph 6:12).

Christ came as the Second Adam. Whereas Adam failed the test in the garden of Eden, Christ passed the test, and dealt with all three of the curses we inherited from Adam (1 Cor 15:45). By our human birth we inherit all Adam's sins and curses, but by being reborn in Christ, we inherit God's blessings of grace and justification, sanctification and righteousness, and eternal life. These blessings can only be inherited through spiritual birth by faith in Jesus Christ alone (John 3:5–6).

Jesus Christ, the Second Adam, passed the test both when he defeated Satan's temptations (Matt 4:1–11); and when he died on the cross, rose from the dead and, ascended into heaven to take his place at the right hand of the Father. His complete and final defeat of Satan and all his angels will take place when he establishes the new heaven, the new earth and the New Jerusalem.

God's Plan of Salvation and Redemption

In Ephesians 1:3–14, the Apostle Paul gives a clear explanation of what redemption in Christ Jesus means. This passage may have been a hymn of praise sung by the first Christians. It celebrates the role of God the Father, God the Son and God the Holy Spirit in the work of redemption. The Father planned it, the Son carried out the plan, and the Holy Spirit helps us to respond to it.

All believers are chosen by the Father

Paul begins by identifying the role God had played in our redemption (Eph 1:3–6). He stresses the blessings God has chosen to give us. These blessings are not material but are the spiritual benefits of Christ's work. They are associated with the "heavenly realms", that is, the unseen world of spiritual realities in which Christians live. African societies have a rich awareness of spiritual realities, but too often we are oppressed by them and live in fear of them. Christians, however, can confidently face unseen spiritual realities knowing that God has given us spiritual blessings that are all we need for salvation and godliness.

Not only does God make spiritual blessings available, but he has also chosen us to receive them. What a privilege! In fact, God chose us in Christ "before the creation of the world" – before ever Adam and Eve fell. He knew what was coming, and he eternally selected some to be saved by believing in Christ. He decreed that coming to faith in Jesus Christ would be the means of our becoming chosen, saved and forgiven. These are the spiritual blessings that God offers those who believe in Christ.

God's purpose is to restore believers to the state human beings enjoyed before the fall, when they were holy and blameless. They will be remade in God's image, and will reflect his holy character in their lives. By doing this, they will bring glory to him. More than that, believers will not only become God's image-bearers, they will also become his sons and daughters. Our Lord Jesus is God's true Son, but we are adopted into his family, as legal children with all the rights and privileges that entails. This special family relationship gives a new understanding of God as a loving Father, who is near and dear to us, rather than unreachable or unapproachable. Belonging to God's family changes our whole perspective, understanding and relationship to God. He is no longer just our Creator, but also our Father and our Redeemer.

As God's children, we are expected to learn from him and obey him. This may take time to accomplish, because we are more used to listening to the directives of our sinful nature. But the Holy Spirit and the word of God will teach us how to live as the children of our Father.

God's decision to adopt us was not forced on him but is rooted solely in his grace. Our status is also not rooted in what we do, but in God's love for us and for his Son. God's eternal plan of salvation, his blessing us, his choosing us, his predestining us, his adopting us – all are rooted in his love for Christ and are made effective in Christ's work of redemption.

All believers are redeemed by the Son

Paul next lists the blessings we have received from Jesus Christ (Eph 1:7–12). The primary one is his work of redemption, which should move us to love, gratitude, thanksgiving and worship. Our Christian life should be a celebration of God's grace in and through Jesus Christ. We should show grace to others because of the grace we have received.

Christ's sacrifice on the cross freed us from the slavery to sin, Satan and death that had come upon us at the fall. In the garden of Eden we lost eternal life through our rebellion against God and became selfish and proud, greedy and full of lusts, and gripped by anxiety and fear. We inherited sin, God's wrath and judgement, his curse and death. But the cross of Christ fulfilled God's legal requirements of justice and righteousness, and opened the doors for us to receive forgiveness, salvation, righteousness and eternal life. He made it possible for us to be reconciled to God.

By giving his own Son to die for us on the cross, God demonstrated his generosity. When it comes to redemption and forgiveness, God is never stingy. No matter what we have done, we can count on the rich abundance of his grace when we come to him for redemption and forgiveness.

The fact that it was "in Christ" that God executed his plan of salvation and "in Christ" that humanity obtains this salvation means that salvation is available only in Christ. No other traditional intermediary from any religion or culture shares this place within "the mystery of his will" (Eph 1:9).

Just as the fall affected more than just human beings, so God's plan of salvation extends to more than just human beings (Rom 8:18–21). It embraces all things in heaven and on earth. At the climax of time, God will repair all that is in chaos, disorder, hostility and conflict, and will bring all things into unity in subjection in Christ (Eph 1:10). Jesus Christ will then rule the entire universe.

But for the present, Christ is the context and centre within which a body of the believers is born, formed and moulded by the Holy Spirit into a community, the church, his body.

All believers are sealed by the Spirit

When a visitor is welcomed into an Igbo village in Nigeria, his host puts a white chalk mark on the back of his wrist. This mark is a sign that this person is entitled to enjoy the same privileges as the rest of the community, and is also entitled to the protection of the entire community. This sign is similar to the "seal" God puts on believers in the form of the Holy Spirit (Eph 1:13–14). The presence of the Spirit is a sign that they are God's possessions, regardless of what clan or community they belonged to before. All believers share the same status and the same inheritance. They are all united by their shared faith in Christ.

Note that "in Christ". It is not faith in itself that saves. It is possible to have faith in all kinds of things. No, what counts is full acceptance of the truth of the gospel of Christ. All who have this faith share a common mark of identity, namely the Holy Spirit. The Spirit seals us as God's possessions and guarantees our inheritance. He is the down payment that guarantees that we will receive our full inheritance when the day of Christ comes. He is also the one who applies the benefits of redemption in our lives.

Christ's Work of Reconciliation

The traditional African world view was dominated by the pursuit of wholeness and cosmic harmony. But these could never be achieved through African Traditional Religion. Rituals designed to harness the life force cannot give life. The spirit power sought in traditional religion is only a counterfeit of the real power of the Holy Spirit. Cosmic harmony was an unattainable goal.

But Christ offers the way to harmony. In place of the failed attempts to reconcile the natural world, the spirit world and the human world in African Traditional Religion, we have the wonderful reconciliation accomplished by Christ. His death on the cross laid the foundation of salvation and redemption, repentance and forgiveness, peace, love, grace, justice and reconciliation. His work of reconciliation applies to four sets of relationships:

- *Reconciliation between God and human beings.* After the fall, we were all in rebellion against God, and so subject to his judgement. His curse was on us. But through the cross of Christ we now have access to God and can find peace with God and forgiveness (Rom 5:1–2, 8–11; 8:1). The curse has been lifted. If we come to God in faith and repentance, he will receive us.

- *Reconciliation between people.* By dying on the cross, Christ destroyed the enmity that had long existed between Jews and Gentiles. The walls that divided them were abolished (Eph 2:11–22). In the same way, he breaks down all the walls and barriers we have erected against others. He has made us all one in him, as his adopted brothers and sisters. There is no longer any room for hatred, prejudice, stereotyping, discrimination and bias. In Christ a new humanity has been created in which "there is neither Jew nor Gentile, neither slave nor free, nor is there male and female, for you are all one in Christ Jesus" (Gal 3:28). Peace now reigns as opposed to conflict, violence and hatred.

- *Reconciliation between spirit, soul and body.* As we have seen, the fall resulted in our experiencing inner conflict as our spirit, soul and body forgot the natural order and competed for supremacy. But when we come to Christ, the sinful nature that encouraged these conflicts is nailed to the cross with him. When we surrender our spirit, soul and

body to God, he restores the correct order and we can live in peace and harmony with ourselves.
- *Restoration of God's fallen creation.* At the fall, God pronounced a curse on creation. This curse, too, was broken on the cross, and all creation will be restored to a state of harmony (Col 1:19–22; 2 Cor 5:19; Rom 8:18–22). In the book of Revelation the Apostle John describes the coming destruction of the present fallen creation to make way for a new earth and a new heaven. The chief actor in this work of re-creation is our Lord himself, whose victory on the cross has made him the Prince of Peace, the Righteous Judge, and the Ruler over all the universe (Rev 4, 5).

The traditional African quest for spirit power in the cosmos and in life finds its ultimate fulfilment in Christ's work of reconciliation. He has conquered and soundly defeated all the spiritual and mysterious forces and powers that dominate the universe. Our lives need no longer be dominated by fear of spirit power. Christ the Victor offers deliverance and hope.

The Resurrection Power of Jesus

There is an African saying, "A great man is not one who falls and dies, but one who rises from the dead." Through his death and resurrection, Jesus Christ has overthrown all the satanic powers that are associated with evil, sin and death. Even before his death, he asserted his power over death in the raising of Lazarus (John 11:25–26). The writer of the letter to the Hebrews describes Christ's plan as being that "by his death he might break the power of him who holds the power of death – that is, the devil – and free those who all their lives were held in slavery by their fear of death" (Heb 2:14–15). He announces that he has accomplished this when he appears to the Apostle John on Patmos, proclaiming "Do not be afraid; I am the First and the Last. I am the Living One; I was dead, and now look, I am alive for ever and ever! And I hold the keys of death and Hades" (Rev 1:17b–18; see also 1 Cor 15).

But even though Christ has "disarmed the powers and authorities [and] made a public spectacle of them, triumphing over them by the cross" (Col 2:15) traditional Africans still turn to spirit beings, mystical and unseen powers and forces for help, guidance, and protection. They have got a completely wrong answer to the key questions of life: Who controls this universe? Who maintains this universe? Who will give us protection, guidance, sustenance, comfort and peace? These questions address God's sovereignty, providence and wisdom. The correct answer to all of them is – Christ!

The power of the cross of Jesus must be applied to the spiritual and dynamic realities of African life. African spirit power is sustained by the blood of animals and birds and sometimes even by human blood. These blood sacrifices generate powerful spiritual forces in those who practice them. The only power that can break this traditional power is the blood of Jesus Christ shed on the cross. Even greater than the power of his blood is the power of his resurrection.

The spiritual forces and powers in Africa know the power of Jesus Christ, even if many Africans do not. We have all heard how the pioneering missionaries in Africa confronted and overcame the power of traditional African spirits, ancestors, gods and divinities with the power of Jesus Christ. Even witchcraft, sorcery and divination were no match for the resurrection power of Jesus Christ. But the church in Africa has forgotten this. We need to recover the understanding that the apostles and the pioneering missionaries had of God's

> incomparably great power for us who believe. That power is the same as the mighty strength he exerted when he raised Christ from the dead and seated him at his right hand in the heavenly realms, far above all rule and authority, power and dominion and every name that is invoked, not only in the present age but also in the one to come. (Eph 1:19–21)

The Church, the Body of Christ

One physical manifestation of Christ's salvation is the formation by the work of the Holy Spirit of the new messianic community, the church. The traditional African's longing for a kinship community is fulfilled in this community, in which Christ breaks down tribal differences, barriers and divisions and creates a new humanity, centred on himself.

Water baptism is the means of initiating new believers into the church. It is the physical and social manifestation of what the Holy Spirit did when they came to conversion and faith in Jesus Christ. The same route applies to all, regardless of their ethnic or educational background (1 Cor 12:12) for this new community transcends any human classification by race, tribe, nationality, etc. In this new community, there are no strangers or aliens, only brothers and sisters in Christ. Their inward baptism of the Holy Spirit and their outward water baptism seal their new identity, unity and oneness. From now on, they are to live as a family in love and unity. They cannot bring their old attitudes and prejudices into this new messianic community.

The inner transformation of people who become followers of Jesus should have great social implications. It should affect the societies in which they live. They should show others the mercy, grace, love, peace and forgiveness they have received in everyday life.

The model for their life and character is Jesus. Just as Jesus came to serve and bless others, even those who rejected him, so the church should serve and bless others. The traditional kinship values of affinity, loyalty and obligations no longer only apply within the community but also apply to the way the community interacts with those who are outside it. Christians should respond not only to the needs of fellow believers but also to the needs of the whole world. The love that all the members of the new community show each other should become their distinguishing mark and itself bear testimony to Christ's redemptive work (John 17:21–23).

The new community does not exist for its own sake but for Christ and humanity. It has no right to decide who joins it and who does not. It is the prerogative of the Father to choose who comes to faith and joins his church. The good news of the gospel, which is an invitation to join this community, is to be offered to all, without discrimination. Ethnic differences should not be exploited for selfish purposes but should be transformed and redeemed so that we can use our different strengths to serve humanity in the name of Christ.

Christ's example is the compelling reason for seeking to reach "outsiders" and "strangers" with the good news of Christ. Christ himself set everything else aside while he searched for his lost sheep. We should do no less.

But while the new messianic community must challenge traditional understandings of community, it must also challenge the contemporary understanding of community, which is framed in terms of secularism, pluralism and modernism. A community with Christ as its head cannot be secular. A community that is focused on Christ cannot include those who refuse to acknowledge him. But while these people may not become members of the community, they must still be served by the community. Every attempt must be made to lovingly invite both traditional and modern Africans, and men and women of all religions and cultures, into the community. They should be touched by our dedication, motivation and love, which break down the barriers people erect against Christ.

Like the ethnic and tribal conflicts in Africa, the social, moral, economic and political corruption and decay in Africa are also rooted in human sin. But in the church, Christ is creating a new community for a new humanity, re-created in Christ Jesus who restores what sin has destroyed.

12

APPLYING THE POWER OF THE CROSS OF CHRIST

There is an African saying, "Lack of knowledge makes a visitor drink washing water." Another says, "A sick man is not cured by holding a gourd of medicine, but by drinking it." These sayings hold true when it comes to applying the power of the cross to the problem of sin. Many Christians don't know how to do this.

In the previous chapter, I sketched out the great work that Christ has done on the cross. But some of you may be wondering how that applied to the specific topic of this book. In this chapter, I will answer that question, explaining how the cross of Christ deals with both our sinful nature and our sinful acts.[69]

God the Son & self-centredness and pride

God the Holy Spirit & greed and lust

God the Father & anxiety and fear

Response of the Triune God

Sins and Sin

The word "sin" is used in two ways in the Apostle Paul's letters. When it is used in the singular, "sin" usually refers to the sinful nature we inherited from Adam. This root sin corrupts everything we do. In Romans 5:12–8:12, Paul discusses the origin, nature, power and effect of our sinful nature and how to deal with its effects on us.

The fruit of this sinful nature are the sinful acts we commit and our sinful attitudes to others. These are our sins (plural). Paul discusses these sins in Romans 1–5:11.

Sins and personal guilt

We have all done things that were motivated by self-centredness and pride, greed and lust, or sinful anxiety and fear. We are all aware that we have broken God's moral laws in some way. Thus we are all lawbreakers. As such, we all stand guilty before God, our Maker and Creator, and deserve to be judged and punished by him. None of us can deny this, for we all know that we are responsible for our own behaviour.

Our awareness of our guilt makes us fear God. What can we do to deflect his anger? How can we possibly obtain forgiveness? How can we escape the dreadful truth that "the wages of sin is death" (Rom 6:23).

Our only hope is to turn to the cross, where Christ dealt with our sins (plural). All that we need to do is confess our sinful behaviour, acts, deeds, attitudes and practices. All of these will be forgiven if we confess them, for the Apostle John assures us: "he is faithful and will forgive us our sins and purify us from all unrighteousness" (1 John 1:9).

All who turn to Christ and confess their sins receive forgiveness, deliverance from the punishment they deserve (Rom 1–5:12); and access to God's holy presence (Rom 5:1–2). We no longer need to live in fear of God! We no longer need to dread his punishment. Jesus Christ on the cross paid the full penalty for us and we can go free.

As believers we have redemption through the blood of Jesus Christ and forgiveness of sins through his blood (Eph 1:7). But while many Christians are eager to accept redemption, they are much less interested in experiencing forgiveness. They do not confess their sins to God, and consequently they do not receive forgiveness, or experience sanctification and spiritual growth. Confession is not something that can be done once for all, but is something we need to do regularly in order to deal with the sins that spring up like weeds in our daily life. If we do not deal with these weeds, and apply the benefits of the cross to our sin problem, we are only half-alive in Christ, and not enjoying the full blessings of salvation.

Sin and inherited corruption

The reason we all commit sins is that we all have sinful natures. We inherited these from our forefathers, who disobeyed God in the garden of Eden. When self-centredness and pride led them to reject God and choose to follow their own path, they set our feet on a path that led us away from God too. We all share the guilt of the sin (singular) which is now our second nature. Our sinful nature now controls and dominates our life and leads us to commit acts of sin.

How do we deal with this inherited corruption? Is the solution the same as for the sins we actually commit? Can we confess that we have a sinful nature and be forgiven, just as we are for the sins we commit? That seems unlikely, because true repentance and confession require that we turn away from our sin. But how can we turn away from who we are? How do we change our very natures? How can we deal with this tyrant and bully who drives us crazy and causes us to commit sinful acts? We need deliverance, not just forgiveness, if we are ever to be able to have fellowship with a sinless and holy God.

Fortunately, the Bible does tell us how to gain deliverance from our sinful nature:

- *Crucifixion.* The first step involves a drastic action – dying, for "anyone who has died has been set free from sin" (Rom 6:7). Our sinful nature needs to be crucified, or put to death. Exactly how this takes place is a mystery, but what we do know is that on the cross Jesus took on himself the sinful nature that had come upon all humanity through Adam's sin. The Son of God "who had no sin" was "made sin for us" (2 Cor 5:21). When we turn to Christ in faith and believe in him, our old self is crucified with him on the cross. The power of our sinful nature is broken. It is not that we suddenly become perfectly sinless, for crucifixion is a slow death, but the cross weakens the death grip that our sinful nature has on our character. Once we have crucified our sinful nature, we are free to begin to live the type of life that Paul is referring to when he says that "sin shall no longer be your master" (Rom 6:14). Paul explains this in some detail in Romans 6, 7 and 8, where he explains how "our old self was crucified with him so that the body ruled by sin might be done away with, that we should no longer be slaves to sin" (Rom 6:6). Or in other words, "I have been crucified with Christ and I no longer live, but Christ lives in me" (Gal 2:20).

- *Sanctification*. Once we have crucified our sinful nature, the Holy Spirit moves in and he applies the power of the cross and the word of God in our life in a process that we call sanctification. It involves the daily eradication of the influence of sin in our lives. For sanctification to be effective, we have to crucify our selves daily, and daily apply the power of the cross to our life. We have to remind ourselves not only that our old sinful self was crucified with Jesus, but also that we have been raised with him and are now "alive to God in Christ Jesus" (Rom 6:11). This is a spiritual resurrection, rather than a physical one (although it foreshadows our future physical resurrection at Christ's return). This can be a difficult concept for some to grasp. Even the educated Nicodemus struggled when Jesus told him,

  > Flesh gives birth to flesh, but the Spirit gives birth to spirit. You should not be surprised at my saying, "You must be born again". The wind blows wherever it pleases. You hear its sound, but you cannot tell where it comes from or where it is going. So it is with everyone born of the Spirit. (John 3:6–8)

- *Washing and Cleansing*. When Adam and Eve sinned, they became aware of their nakedness and experienced shame and anxiety. They recognized the stains and shame of their sinful nature. These stains are still on us, until our nature is washed, cleansed and purified by the blood of the Lamb. We are already being washed clean through the Holy Spirit who lives in us, but at the consummation of our salvation at the Lord's second coming, we shall be fully cleansed and clothed in God's glory, righteousness and holiness, just as Adam and Eve were before the fall.

Spiritual Death and Resurrection

After reading what has been said above, you may be asking, "Why do we believers still struggle with sin if Christ's death on the cross gives us victory over sins and delivers us from our sinful nature?" This is a good question.

The first step toward answering it is to recognize that the cross of Jesus Christ did not immediately eradicate sin or evil from the world. If he had done this, there would be no sin anywhere in the world. But sin is still with us until the day of judgement and the coming of the new heaven and the new earth and the kingdom of God (Rev 19–22).

Nor did the cross transform us so that we are no longer human beings with human bodies. No. Our human body has not been eradicated by the cross. Our identification with Christ in his death, burial and resurrection is spiritual, not physical. We are still in the physical bodies that have come to us through our descent from Adam. And all our lives, our fallen soul has directed our spirit and body to act in ways that fulfil its sinful desires. It is eager to carry on doing this. When temptation comes in the form of external forces encouraging us to sin, the old sinful nature tries to respond.

It is not our body as such that is tempted, because sin does not communicate with the body. There is no communication between what is spiritual and what is non-spiritual. Our body is non-spiritual and does not communicate with temptation. But external evil and sin still communicate with the old self and soul and spirit, and try to get us to act in ways that fulfil its sinful desires. Thus we are still vulnerable to temptation.

So what does it mean to say that our old nature has died and that we now live in Christ? It means that instead of being heirs of Adam, deserving God's wrath and judgement and death, we are heirs of Christ, and have been promised grace, righteousness, forgiveness and eternal life. These spiritual blessings become ours when we accept by faith that Jesus died and rose for us, and that we have died and risen with him into a new life in Christ. Our rebirth is not a physical birth but a spiritual one by faith and through the Holy Spirit.

We must be careful not to think of this work of the Holy Spirit as being like gaining access to the life force or spirit power that is so important in the African concept of dynamism. The Holy Spirit is not a force to be controlled by rituals or spiritual formulas. He is a person who creates in us the life of God at our conversion and acceptance of Jesus Christ.

In 1 Corinthians 15 Paul gives a fuller explanation of the meaning of the resurrection of Jesus Christ. Jesus rose from the dead with a new body, a resurrection body (1 Cor 15: 44–49). This body is similar to the one we will receive in Christ and is the body in which Jesus went back to heaven (Acts 1:9–11). After his ascension, Jesus sent his followers the Holy Spirit, who takes Christ's place and works with his people until Christ returns at his second coming. It is the Holy Spirit who gives us the new self or new life in Christ. That is why he is called the "the Spirit who gives life" (Rom 8:2). The uncreated Holy Spirit comes to live within believers. He replaces our disposition to sin with God's grace that enables us to do acts of righteousness. He conforms us to the likeness of Christ. He creates God's love in us for both God and fellow human beings. He directs, controls, enables and motivates us to obey Christ, so that we can produce the fruit of the Spirit (Gal 5:22–23) and the fruit of righteousness (Col 3:12–17; Rom 5:1–5; 2 Pet 1:5–11) and the fruit of light (Eph 5:8–9). The Holy Spirit cannot be tempted to sin.

What does this mean for how we deal with temptation? It means that we have to respond spiritually. The Apostle Paul says, "count yourselves dead to sin but alive to God in Christ Jesus" (Rom 6:11). This is a statement of faith. By faith we must believe that our old self has been crucified with Jesus Christ and that we have been spiritually reborn by putting our faith in Jesus Christ. This faith must be consistent, a moment by moment believing and trusting, a moment by moment crucifixion of our old self, a moment by moment deliverance from the power and influence of sin – not allowing sin to reign in our bodies to make us obey its evil desires (Rom 6:12–14), a moment by moment confession of our acts of sins, and a moment by moment yielding to the live-giving Spirit. Instead of being ruled by our dead old self, we must serve a new master, the Holy Spirit, and live under the "law of the Spirit who gives life" (Rom 8:1–12). Under the power of the Holy Spirit, our spirit now assumes rule over our soul (will, mind and emotions) and our body.

Yes. Sin is still in the world, but we are no longer its slaves. We have been set free. Our old self is dead. We are not married to a dead person, but to a living life-giving Spirit who is our new Master. The Holy Spirit creates the life of Christ in us and conforms us to the image of God's Son (Rom 8:29). We are now slaves to God's righteousness (Rom 6:19) and no longer slaves to sin (Rom 6:12–14).

Spiritual Death and Remarriage

Paul has been using death and resurrection as metaphors for our new life in Christ. Later in Romans he uses the metaphor of marriage to explain what is happening and why we still struggle with sin (Rom 7:1–6). He is talking about God's law, which is "holy, righteous and good" (Rom 7:12) but which we find we cannot obey. The reason we cannot obey is because we have sinful natures and thus constantly find ourselves condemned by the law. It is almost as if we are married to our old self. It is an unhappy marriage, but we cannot get free of it. The only way to escape such a marriage is for the one partner to die.

When Christ took on our sinful nature and died on the cross, it is as if we were set free from our terrible marriage to sin. We are now free to marry someone else – and that someone else is the resurrected Jesus, who wants us to become his bride. We joyfully enter this marriage – but sometimes we hear the voice of our former husband whispering in our ears. Sometimes we listen to that voice, and not to the voice of our new husband. We are acting as if the old husband is still alive when we obey his instructions to sin. We have to remind ourselves that he has been put to death and that now our only loyalty should be to Christ.

When Christians who are married to Christ act in sinful ways that reveal the influence of their former husband, they are showing that they are not free of his influence. This is a problem that we all struggle with, for none of us live in conformity with the nature of our new husband and in perfect obedience to the holy and perfect law of God. In fact we find it impossible to do this. But this is where our new husband steps in. Through his death and resurrection, he has set us free from the past. He now gives us his Holy Spirit, who gives us a new life in which we will begin to find that we cannot tolerate sin anymore. We will no longer be focused on what our sinful nature desires, but on what God desires. What we could not do on our own, we can do through the power of the Holy Spirit (Rom 8:1–12).

Conclusion

We have seen how God has provided a way to deal with our sinful nature and with the sins to which it gives rise. The challenge to us is to make full use of this great gift that God has given us by sending his Son to bear our sins on the cross. There Christ died once and for all. This single act has eternal value and was done once for all. However, our acceptance of this gift is not done once and for all. We need to go back to the cross daily to crucify ourselves and receive cleansing, forgiveness and deliverance.

In the next three chapters, we will show how to apply the power of the cross of Christ to the three pairs of root sins described earlier in the book.

13

SELF-CENTREDNESS, PRIDE AND THE CROSS

The first pair of root sins we identified were self-centredness and pride. In this chapter, we will look at how to deal with the sins that spring from this root pair.

Dealing with the Self

Sin is rooted in the self. The entire self has been infected by sin. We are born sinners, and because of that, we sin. In the previous chapter, we dealt at length with how God deals with our sinful nature and with the requirement that the self be put to death in order for us to receive a fresh life from the Spirit of God. There is no other way of solving the problem of sin and the self except the way of the cross. Christ died on the cross for us, and we in turn must take up our cross and follow him.

Denying ourselves

Anyone who wishes to be a disciple or a follower of Jesus must heed his teaching on self-denial.

> Whoever wants to be my disciple must deny themselves and take up their cross daily and follow me. For whoever wants to save their life will lose it, but whoever loses their life for me will save it. What good is it for someone to gain the whole world, and yet lose or forfeit their very self? (Luke 9:23–25)

To be a follower of Jesus requires that we must make a radical decision to deny ourselves on a daily basis, living each day, not for self, but for Christ. We are to crucify the self with its pride and sins that stand in the way of service to the Master. This is a wise choice, for those who lose their lives, whether through martyrdom or disciplined self-denial, will find them in the age to come. But those who insist on living for themselves and refusing to submit to the Lordship of Christ will lose their "self" in the age to come. Clinging to one's life results in losing the very self one wants to preserve.

Jesus' teaching sounds even more startling when he says, "If anyone comes to me and does not hate father and mother, wife and children, brothers and sisters – yes, even their own life – such a person cannot be my disciple. And whoever does not carry their cross and follow me cannot be my disciple" (Luke 14:25–27; see also Matt 10:37).

Jesus is not saying that we must neglect our social responsibilities. Of course, we must love our families. But he is telling us to get our priorities straight. Family or social issues must not take precedence over our loyalty and service to our Lord and Master. In fact, very often our concerns for our family and community are tainted with our own self-interest. Jesus demands self-denial and self-sacrifice if we are to become his true followers and disciples.

Mortifying the flesh

Mortifying simply means putting to death all sinful deeds and thoughts in order to weaken the power of sin in our life. Paul tells us to "Put to death, therefore, whatever belongs to your earthly nature: sexual immorality, impurity, lust, evil desires and greed, which is idolatry" (Col 3:5).

We cannot do this in our own strength. But we are able to do so through the Holy Spirit, who is given to those who believe in God's redemption accomplished in the cross of Christ. Paul illustrated this in Romans chapters 7 and 8. We humans are not able to keep God's holy laws because of our sinful nature. We know what we should do, but are unable to do it. So God provided a solution to this problem. When we believe in Jesus and his work of redemption on the cross, we receive a new birth through the Holy Spirit. The Holy Spirit places in believers in Christ the new law of the Spirit of life who delivers us from the law of sin and death. The Holy Spirit then does the work of mortification in us. That is why Paul can say that "if by the Spirit you put to death the misdeeds of the body, you will live" (Rom 8:13).

So far we have discussed ways of dealing with the sin problem of self through the cross and the teachings of Jesus and Paul on self-denial and mortification. But solving the problem of pride which we raised in the previous chapter takes a different approach.

Dealing with Pride

Self and pride are closely related, for pride is the outward manifestation of the sinfulness of the self. But because pride manifests itself in a different way, it has to be dealt with differently. This is an important principle to note. Not all sin problems have the same solution. The solution will vary according to the nature of the sin.

When the root sin of pride affects our spirit, soul and body, it results in the types of sins listed on p. 88. These attitudes and behaviours are often referred to as the works of the flesh. The flesh, like the self, is dealt with only through crucifixion. Thus these sinful attitudes and actions are to be put to death. Pride itself, however, is not to be crucified but is to be confessed and renounced. Those who have received victory over sin through the cross of Jesus Christ must learn how to live new lives in which they walk in humility before God and before all others.

Confessing our pride

In a previous chapter the sin of pride was characterized by statements such as: "I will ascend". "I will exalt myself". "I will sit on the mount". "I will be like God". Pride is always characterized by an arrogant lifting up of oneself above all others, and supremely against God when we refuse to submit to him. We all need deliverance from this sin. Our pride must be laid aside. We need to confess it and renounce it. But we are powerless to do so through our own strength or wisdom. All we can do is confess our sins of pride, receive God's forgiveness and be cleansed through the shed blood of Christ on the cross.

But we need something to replace the spirit of pride, and that is what Jesus Christ offers us. His spirit of humility counters the satanic spirit of pride.

Becoming a servant

Humility is the antidote for pride. It is the only effective means of dealing with it. It is the exact opposite of the spirit expressed in the four "I will's" in the previous section. It follows Jesus, who in the Garden of Gethsemane, three times said, "Not as I will, but as you will" (Matt 26:36–44).[70] Jesus also said that his food or desire was to do the will of the Father (John 4:34; 6:38; 17:4). He subordinated his own will to that of the Father. As his followers, we can do no less than submit to the supreme will of God.

Jesus demonstrated humility not only in relation to God but also in relation to other people. He treated them with meekness, gentleness, compassion and love. He modelled humility and servanthood to his disciples (Matt 11:29; Mark 10:42–45; John 13:4–17). He taught that greatness is earned only through humble service. The one desiring to be first should be the last, and the one desiring to be the greatest should be the least, the servant of all. The one desiring to be served should be the one serving.

Jesus established the law of humility: "The greatest among you will be your servant. For those who exalt themselves will be humbled, and those who humble themselves will be exalted" (Matt 23:12; see also Luke 14:11; 18:14). He places the position, role and function of a slave at the centre of his teachings and ministry. The only duty of a slave is to serve. Being on the lowest rung of society, a slave can never feel too important to serve someone else. Service is the natural language of a slave.

Think what a difference it would make in Africa if our leaders, rulers and elders were to imbibe the spirit of Christ and practice humility and service as their chief virtues. Think what a difference it would make in our own lives if we and those around us were no longer filled with pride and selfishness and stopped trying to lord it over others. This is what Jesus vehemently denounced in all leaders. True service to others can only be done in the spirit of humility. And true greatness and true leadership can only be achieved through humble service.

Imitating Christ

Paul presents Christ as the model for all believers, telling us to "do nothing out of selfish ambition or vain conceit. Rather, in humility value others above yourselves, not looking to your own interests but each of you to the interests of the others" (Phil 2:3–4). Then Paul went on to show what it means to be humble like Christ by reminding us of how much Christ humbled himself for us: 1) he left heaven's glory, 2) he made himself of no reputation, 3) he was made in human likeness, 4) he humbled himself, 5) he became obedient to death, and 6) he died an accursed death on the cross (Phil 2:5–8). What a contrast between this attitude and Satan's self-exaltation! What a rebuke to our own pride!

The Apostle Peter also held up the humility of Christ as an example for all believers. "When they hurled their insults at him, he did not retaliate; when he suffered, he made no threats. Instead, he entrusted himself to him who judges justly" (1 Pet 2:23). The spirit of humility is also the spirit of submission. A proud spirit can never be submissive. Its pride can never take insults. And its arrogance can never bow down before authority.

Paul himself models what it means to imitate the humility of Christ:

> But whatever were gains to me I now consider loss for the sake of Christ. What is more, I consider everything a loss because of the surpassing worth of knowing Christ Jesus my Lord, for whose sake I have lost all things. I consider them garbage, that I may gain Christ and be found in him, not having a righteousness of my own that comes from the law, but that which is through faith in Christ – the righteousness that comes from God on the basis of faith. (Phil 3:7–9)

We are to become like Jesus. Like him, we must show humility, meekness, gentleness, submission and servanthood in how we treat others.

Summary

The only way to deal with the problem of self and pride in human life is for the old self to die and be replaced by a new self in Christ Jesus. We will then be able to live a new life in which we daily deny ourselves and follow in the footsteps of our Lord by serving others, rather than expecting them to serve us.

Jesus death on the cross gives deliverance and enables us to be forgiven for our selfishness and pride. That was a once-and-for-all historical event. But since we are still in our sinful human bodies, we still have to crucify our self and our flesh daily. As we apply Jesus' teachings on self-denial, self-sacrifice and humility, the power and influence of sin and the works of the flesh will weaken. We will become stronger in our fight against the works of the sinful self in our life and will become more like the type of people God meant us to be, people who can have a good influence on the social and moral lives of those around us.

14

GREED, LUST AND THE CROSS

Without the Spirit of God, we are like cars without petrol. We cannot function properly. We are like boats without rudders. We cannot steer in the right direction. We are left with a spiritual void, which greed and lust frantically attempt to fill. The sins of greed dominate our body, while those of lust dominate our soul. Lacking spiritual food, we feed our appetites to the point of gluttony; lacking living water, we seek to quench our spiritual thirst with alcohol; lacking true joy, we indulge in fleeting pleasures. But regardless of what we do, we remain spiritually bankrupt. The needs of greed and lust are insatiable. No amount of food, drink or pleasure will ever be enough to fill the spiritual void caused by the lack of a relationship with God.

We have seen how Jesus Christ has made it possible for us to be restored to a relationship with God and has dealt with both our sinful nature and the sins we commit. He took our fallen self in his human body and nailed it to the cross, effectively destroying the power of our sinful nature. He is our master, our teacher and our role model when it comes to dealing the sins caused by self-centredness and pride. But when it come to the sins of greed and lust, our attention must turn to the role of the Third Person of the Trinity, namely the Holy Spirit.

The concept of the Holy Spirit as the Spirit of God is uniquely Christian. There is no equivalent being in African Traditional Religion. True, there are a host of spirit beings, but none of them would ever be spoken of as the spirit of the Supreme Being.

The major task of the Holy Spirit is to apply the benefits of the cross of Christ to all those who are willing to accept God's solution to the problem of sin. He does this through the processes of regeneration and sanctification.

The Holy Spirit and Regeneration

Our spiritual separation from God means we are spiritually dead. But all those who believe in Christ and confess their sins receive God's forgiveness for their inherited sinfulness and for the sins they have committed. They also receive the gift of eternal life through the Holy Spirit, who also comes to dwell within them. Those who were dead in their trespasses and sins are now spiritually alive! They have been reborn. This new birth is referred to as regeneration.

Regeneration and faith

Believers in African Traditional Religion find it hard to accept that all that is required for rebirth is belief in Jesus and his work on the cross. It seems too simple to be true. Surely some additional animal sacrifice or elaborate ritual is needed to access spirit power? The writer of the book of Hebrews addresses this exact question. In chapters 7 to 10 he explains why the sacrifice of Jesus on the cross is far superior to any sacrifice involving animal blood. He states that Christ,

> has appeared once for all at the culmination of the ages to do away with sin by the sacrifice of himself ... Christ was sacrificed once to take away the sins of many; and he will appear a second time, not to bear sin, but to bring salvation to those who are waiting for him. (Heb 9:26–28)

There is no need for any more blood sacrifices or religious ceremonies. What Jesus did on the cross is sufficient to take care of all human sin – past, present and future. There is nothing we can add to it. Paul rightly reminds us "it is by grace you have been saved, through faith – and this is not from yourselves, it is the gift of God – not by works, so that no one can boast" (Eph 2:8–9).

Regeneration and new life

Turning to Christ involves a sorrowful confession of our sinfulness, and a willingness to turn away from sin. Christians also need to confess every time they become aware of some sin in their lives. Many believers do this, but they make the mistake of thinking that is all they need to do. They fail to recognize the deep roots that sin has in our natures. Our bodies are dominated by a host of sins of greed, and our souls by a host of sins of lust. We need to learn how to deal with the sinful works of the flesh in our life. And the only way to do this is to be willing to put the self to death on the cross in preparation for the coming of new life. This is what Paul is speaking of when he says,

> If we have been united with him in a death like his, we will certainly also be united with him in a resurrection like his ... If we died with Christ, we believe that we will also live with him. For we know that since Christ was raised from the dead, he cannot die again; death no longer has mastery over him. The death he died, he died to sin once for all; but the life he lives, he lives to God. In the same way, count yourselves dead to sin but alive to God in Christ Jesus. (Rom 6:5, 8–11)

Being "alive to God" means that sin is no longer our master. We cannot allow sin to reign in our bodies. We cannot obey the evil desires of sin. We are not to use any part of ourselves as "an instrument of wickedness". We have been brought from death to life so that we can live for God. We are to offer the parts of our body to God so that our whole body will be an "instrument of righteousness". We are not to become slaves to sin but have been set free so as to become slaves to righteousness (Rom 6:12–18). Being alive to God means bearing the fruit of righteousness and the fruit of light, namely "all goodness, righteousness and truth" (Eph 5:8–9). It also means bearing the fruit of the Spirit: "love, joy, peace, forbearance, kindness, goodness, faithfulness, gentleness and self-control (Gal 5:22–23). Being alive to God means that we belong to Jesus Christ and have crucified the sinful nature with its passions and desires.

This new life that enables us to live for God was given to us by the Holy Spirit when we believed in the Lord Jesus Christ. We cannot deal with sin in our life through the power of the Holy Spirit unless we are born of God.

Regeneration and eternal life

The life that the Holy Spirit gives us is referred to as eternal life. To understand what this means, we need to return to Genesis. In the garden of Eden, God gave Adam and Eve a choice between life (the Tree of Life) or death (the Tree of the Knowledge of Good and Evil). They chose death and thereby forfeited life. Their sin resulted in spiritual separation from God and ultimately led to both spiritual and physical death. The life that we lost in that garden is what Christ is offering as eternal life. In Adam we inherited sin and death, but in Jesus, the Second Adam, we inherit grace and life eternal.

There are two Greek words for life. One is *bios*, which refers to our ordinary or biological life which is limited, full of infirmities and culminates in death. The other is *zoe*, which refers to a quality of life that goes beyond the ordinary. This is life from God mediated through Jesus Christ and the Holy Spirit, a fulfilled, enhanced, eternal life.[71]

The hope of living beyond *bios* is made certain by the new *zoe* offered by Jesus Christ. He displayed his power to give such life when he called Lazarus, who had been dead for four days, back to life (John 11:25). He demonstrated it supremely in his resurrection.

Zoe is Christ's resurrection life that is given to us in this present life. We do not have to wait to receive it at the second coming of Christ. It is ours the moment we believe in Jesus Christ. We regain what we lost in the garden of Eden. We will know this kind of life in full at the resurrection, but we already experience it in part now, even in this fallen world.

However, although we have new life from God, we still have to deal with our corrupt flesh. Regeneration of our spirit does not eradicate our soul and body. The Holy Spirit has to work with our cooperation to mortify and sanctify them. We have to put them to death on a daily basis.

Nurturing New Life

The believer has to do the work of overcoming the flesh and renewing the mind (Rom 12:2). This involves nurturing the life God has given to us through spiritual birth to prevent it being dominated by sin. For this reason, we need to look at some basic principles of nurturing our new life under God if we are to overcome our bondage to the root sins of greed and lust.

Greed and the bread of life

When Jesus miraculously fed 5,000 people with five loaves of bread and two fish, his purpose was not just to supply them with food but also to make them aware that he is the bread of life. He challenged them:

> Do not work for food that spoils, but for food that endures to eternal life, which the Son of Man will give you ... I am the bread of life. Whoever comes to me will never go hungry, and whoever believes in me will never be thirsty ... For my Father's will is that everyone who looks to the Son and believes in him shall have eternal life, and I will raise them up at the last day. (John 6:27, 35, 40)

There are many people in this world who believe that the purpose of life is nothing more than to be born, eat, drink, die and then be buried. But Jesus offers eternal life beyond this ordinary life for all those who believe in him. He offers a new kind of life which is far superior to what our human greed and lust have to offer us. Our insatiable greed can only be satisfied by eating the bread of life, or in other words by accepting Christ's offer of himself to us.

There is one other source of spiritual food for believers, and that is the word of God. Jesus contrasted it with physical bread when he said that "Man shall not live on bread alone, but on every word that comes from the mouth of God" (Matt 4:4). It convicts us of sin, corrects our ways, confirms our faith, and equips us to lead holy lives before God. That is why the psalmist says, "I have hidden your word in my heart that I may not sin against you" (Ps 119:11). A body that is fed daily with this kind of spiritual food is strengthened against surrendering itself to the works of sin and flesh. Instead, it will produce works of righteousness.

Greed and living water

We humans suffer not only from spiritual hunger but also from a spiritual thirst that nothing material can satisfy. Jesus came to offer us the Holy Spirit who can satisfy our spiritual thirst. He said

> Everyone who drinks this water will be thirsty again, but whoever drinks the water I give them will never thirst. Indeed, the water I give them will become in them a spring of water welling up to eternal life ... If anyone is thirsty, let him come to me and drink. Whoever believes in me, as the Scripture has said, rivers of living water will flow from within them. (John 4:13–14; 7:37–38)

In place of our insatiable greed and lust which are rooted in spiritual hunger and thirst, Jesus offers us himself and the Holy Spirit (for that was what he was referring to when he spoke of living water – John 7:39). Only the bread of life can satisfy our spiritual hunger; only the living water of the Holy Spirit can quench our spiritual thirst.

Lust and the light of the world

After the fall, we were spiritually in total darkness, which leads to spiritual blindness, ignorance and hardness of heart. Paul describes this state in the following words:

> You must no longer live as the Gentiles do, in the futility of their thinking. They are darkened in their understanding and separated from the life of God because of the ignorance that is in them due to the hardening of their hearts. Having lost all sensitivity, they have given themselves over to sensuality so as to indulge in every kind of impurity, and they are full of greed. (Eph 4:17–19)

Christ came to rescue us, but our sins of greed and lust still easily blind us and keep us from seeing and living in the light of God. We prefer to grope around in the dark rather than turning to the one who said, "I am the light of the world. Whoever follows me will never walk in darkness, but will have the light of life" (John 8:12). This was exactly what had been prophesied about him by Isaiah, who said, "The people walking in darkness have seen a great light; on those living in the land of deep darkness a light has dawned" (Isa 9:2). The Apostle John says of him, "In him was life, and that life was the light of all mankind" (John 1:4).

All works of the flesh and sin are works of darkness, from which we can only be delivered by coming to the light. This light is in Jesus, and in the Holy Spirit, and also in the word of God, which the psalmist describes as "a lamp for my feet, a light on my path" (Ps 119:105). We need to learn to walk in this light.

Putting off the works of the flesh

The sins of the body and the sins of the soul comprise the works of flesh, or our sinful nature. This sinful nature is completely opposed to the Holy Spirit. However, Jesus has laid the foundation of our redemption from it, for it was crucified on the cross with him. Now we are the children of God and children of light, and as such we must put off all the works of the flesh and darkness:

> You were taught, with regard to your former way of life, to put off your old self, which is being corrupted by its deceitful desires; to be made new in the attitude of your minds; and to put on the new self, created to be like God in true righteousness and holiness. Therefore each of you must put off falsehood and speak truthfully to your neighbour, for we are all members of one body". (Eph 4:22-24)

This is a command to all believers in Christ. Here, the only specific sin he mentions is lying, but elsewhere Paul gives catalogues of sins that we are to put off. So we need to name our sins and deal with each one by putting it off, or putting it to death:

> Put to death, therefore, whatever belongs to your earthly nature: sexual immorality, impurity, lust, evil desires and greed, which is idolatry. Because of these, the wrath of God is coming. You used to walk in these ways, in the life you once lived. But now you must rid yourselves of all such things as these: anger, rage, malice, slander, and filthy language from your lips. Do not lie to each other, since you have taken off your old self with its practices and have put on the new self, which is being renewed in knowledge in the image of its Creator. (Col 3:5-11; see also Rom 12:9-21; Gal 5:19-22; Eph 4:17-5:14; Col 3:5-11; 2 Tim 3:1-9)

We cannot deal effectively with our sinful deeds and our sinful nature unless God addresses us through the gospel of Christ and calls us to salvation. When we accept the call of God to leave our life of sin and accept Jesus Christ as our Saviour, then God imparts a new life to us through the Holy Spirit. This work of the Holy Spirit is what we call regeneration. God accepts us by giving us a right standing before him. Our sins have been forgiven and we have been justified as if we do not have any sin. We can stand before a holy God on the basis of Christ's righteousness through his cross. God adopts us as his own sons and daughters and makes us members of his family.[72] After this event, we are fully ready for the work of sanctification through the Holy Spirit.

Sanctification and Putting on Christ

In traditional Africa, people think that we can be made holy through blood sacrifices or by observing set times for prayers and fasting, external cleanliness and abstaining from certain food or drinks. Many would want us to believe that it is only when we follow such religious formulas that we can be made holy or righteous.

Christianity, however, insists that what makes us holy is not rituals but the work of the Holy Spirit in our life. He is the one who helps us to grow in holiness as he gradually replaces the corrupted image of God that was disfigured at the fall in Eden with the likeness of Christ. This process of sanctification "is a progressive work of God and man that makes us more and more free from sin and like Christ in our actual lives".[73] It begins when we accept Christ as our Saviour and increases throughout our life until completed at death or when the Lord returns.

Putting on the new self is the exact opposite of putting off all the works of the flesh. The command in Colossians to put on the "new self" is an injunction to cooperate with the work of the Holy Spirit as he indwells us and sets about making us holy and righteous. Our views about life, the way we saw it, the way we understood it, the way we interpreted it before we became Christians, all have to be transformed and renewed so as to conform to the teachings of the word of God and the image of Christ (Rom 8:29).

Paul balances his catalogue of the works of the flesh with a list of the works of righteousness and of the Holy Spirit (Rom 12:9–21; Phil 2:1–5; 4:8–9; Gal 5:16–18, 22–23; Col 3:12–17. We should study these lists and seek to put on these works of righteousness as we walk in the Spirit in a continuous process of sanctification and mortifications of the body of sin.

Walking in the Spirit

The company we keep affects us profoundly. Jesus was well aware of this when he told his disciples that he would send them the Comforter-Counsellor who is the Holy Spirit to keep them company. He would be the guide and teacher to walk alongside them and convict them of sin, righteousness and judgement (John 16:5–14).

The antidote to walking in the flesh is walking in the Spirit, following the law of the Spirit of life rather than the law of sin and death (Rom 8:2). Paul tells us to

> walk by the Spirit, and you will not gratify the desires of the flesh. For the flesh desires what is contrary to the Spirit, and the Spirit what is contrary to the flesh. They are in conflict with each other, so that you are not to do whatever you want. But if you are led by the Spirit, you are not under the law. (Gal 5:16–18)

Our new life in Christ is to be controlled and led by the Holy Spirit. We are no longer slaves to sin but, instead, we are slaves to righteousness and holiness (Rom 6:15–23). We no longer bear the fruits of sin (Gal 5:19–21); instead we bear the fruit of the Spirit (Gal 5:22–23).

There are some important principles of walking in the Spirit that we need to observe. First, we need to confess our sins on a daily basis so as to walk in the light and maintain spiritual fellowship and communion with God and others. The Apostle John reminds us of this:

> God is light; in him there is no darkness at all. If we claim to have fellowship with him and yet walk in the darkness, we lie and do not live out the truth. But if we walk in the light, as he is in the light, we have fellowship with one another, and the blood of Jesus, his Son, purifies us from all sin. If we claim to be without sin, we deceive ourselves and the truth is not in us. If we confess our sins, he is faithful and just and will forgive us

our sins and purify us from all unrighteousness. If we claim we have not sinned, we make him out to be a liar and his word is not in us. (1 John 1:5–10)

Secondly, we need to yield our whole selves to God. This involves shunning the works of sin, allowing our minds to be renewed and transformed daily through the word of God and prayer (Rom 12:1–2) and yielding our bodies to do works of righteousness (Rom 6:13). We are to be dedicated instruments for God's service.

Thirdly, we need to be repeatedly filled and controlled by the Holy Spirit. This filling is maintained by regular confession of sin and yielding ourselves to God completely (Acts 4:31). Our goal as Christians is to be Spirit-filled and to exhibit a Christ-like character, as summed up in the passage on the fruit of the Spirit (Gal 5:22–23).

Summary

Greed and lust produce the sinful works of the flesh. We thus need to be aware of their influence in our life so that we can effectively deal with them. This can only be done through the Holy Spirit's applying God's solution to our greed (the sins of the body) and lust (the sins of the soul). His work of regeneration and sanctification is aimed at reforming and renewing men and women who were dead in trespasses and sins but who have been brought back into a relationship with God through the work of Christ on the cross, the Holy Spirit and the word of God.

The Holy Spirit who lives in us directs us to walk and live according to his ways. The holiness and righteousness he imparts weakens and replaces our sinful desires, passions, sensualities and pleasures.

15

ANXIETY, FEAR AND THE CROSS

The root sin of anxiety and fear first manifested itself when Adam and Eve realized that they were naked and sinful. They had been created in the glorious image of God, but now their very nature had become sinful. Ashamed and guilty, they sewed fig leaves together to cover their nakedness and hid from God. Their descendants now live in a constant state of anxiety and shame, fear and guilt.

We have good reason for these emotions. Our relationship with God has been severed and we now live under his judgement. The whole of creation has turned against us. We are left on our own to face our weakness and finitude.

Realization of Our Creaturehood

We humans are not only sinners by nature, we are also transgressors by practice. Our awareness of this generates all kinds of anxiety and fear as we struggle to deal with our conscience and the disease of sin which affects our life. We also have to live with our creatureliness, or in other words with our vulnerability in this fallen world.

> Men are also deeply troubled by anxious fears arising from their weakness as creatures. The feeling of dependence and contingency, of being subject to uncontrollable forces, form the content of one of these anxieties. The experience

of temporality and mortality, of an approaching dateline to one's powers and life, forms the frightening content of the other.[74]

We cannot solve our own problems and we have lost God's perfect care over us and fellowship with us. No wonder we are haunted by many forms of anxiety and fear.

Yet another reason we are anxious is that we have lost the reason and purpose for our existence. We were created for the sole purpose of worshipping, serving and living in loyalty to our Creator, but we have abandoned this primary duty to our Creator and replaced it with self-made duties that do not satisfy, no matter what we do. We now live in exile, without the harmony and peace that come from a relationship with a sovereign God.

Not only has our relationship with our Maker been broken, so have our relationships with our community, with nature, and with ourselves. All of these broken relationships represent forms of alienation. Our loneliness and lack of fellowship and protection drive us to create our own sources of security. We abandon our Maker and set up surrogate gods and saviours that plunge us further into idolatry and false worship of creatures.

To sum up our situation after the fall, we stand in dire need of 1) reconciliation as regards all broken relationships; 2) protection or cover as regards all forces of evil, principalities and powers that threaten life and existence; 3) restoration and salvation as regards death, curses, catastrophes, suffering, diseases and fate; and 4) authority, order, peace and rest as regards chaos, crises and conflicts.

But God has not abandoned his prodigal children. The cross of Jesus Christ offers reconciliation, restoration and protection to rebellious and disobedient sinners.

Jesus Christ is the one who deals with our self-centredness and pride, the Holy Spirit deals with our greed and lust, and God the Father deals with our anxiety and fear. He does this by bringing us under his rule, dominion, authority, security and sovereignty. All the scriptural injunctions, "do not be afraid", "do not worry", "do not be anxious", are God's warnings against the destructive sins of anxiety and fear.

Restoration and Reconciliation in the Cross of Christ

In traditional Africa, reconciliation of warring factions required elaborate rituals, sacrifices and the shedding of blood. By shedding his own blood, Christ has eliminated the need for such rituals. He has become the Mediator between God and humanity (1 Tim 2:5) and the one who makes peace between warring factions like the Jews and Gentiles (Eph 2:11–19). God's work of reconciliation is thus rooted in the cross of Christ through which rebellious, estranged and alienated people are reconciled with God, with their fellow human beings, with nature and finally with themselves.

When we recognize that we are rebellious and disobedient sinners, repent and confess our sins, God forgives us on the basis of Christ's work on the cross. Both confession and forgiveness of sins are rooted in the finished work of Christ on the cross. Our repentance and God's forgiveness effect reconciliation and restoration. Our broken relationship with God is restored. We return back to our Maker and worship him alone.

Our broken relationship with God was the source of our anxiety and fear, but with the restoration of that relationship we can again enjoy peace, fellowship and communion with God. We no longer have an urge to seek protection, security and provision from lesser gods or spirit beings. God alone is all sufficient. He controls and contains the universe.

Reconciliation with God also brings reconciliation with others. No longer do we need to fear them and see them as enemies. The despair, worry, distrust, corruption and conflict that poisoned our relationships is laid aside as we find reconciliation and peace in the cross of Christ.

The cross of Christ also brought about reconciliation with nature. We were created by God to act as stewards of the world he had created. We were to care for the earth and not destroy it or misuse it. The extent to which fallen humanity has failed to carry out this task is evident in the rising tide of climate change, depletion of natural resources, and the increasing number of endangered or extinct species. All of these are caused by humanity's reckless destruction of ecological systems. Moreover, creation as a whole is still suffering under God's judgement and curse. The cross did not remove the sin, ruin and curse, but it has begun to break their powers. Along with believers, creation eagerly awaits the last day when it will be fully delivered from its suffering. Paul puts it like this:

> The creation waits in eager expectation for the children of God to be revealed. For the creation was subjected to frustration, not by its own choice, but by the will of the one who subjected it, in hope that the creation itself will be liberated from its bondage to decay and brought into the glorious freedom of the children of God. We know that the whole creation has been groaning as in the pains of childbirth right up to the present time. Not only so, but we ourselves, who have the firstfruits of the Spirit, groan inwardly as we wait eagerly for our adoption to sonship, the redemption of our bodies. For in this hope we were saved. But hope that is seen is no hope at all. Who hopes for what he already has? But if we hope for what we do not yet have, we wait for it patiently. (Rom 8:19–25)

As a result of sin, we are also alienated from ourselves. We saw this when we looked at the impact of sin on our essential human nature and at the conflict that has arisen between spirit, soul and body. The cross of Christ and the gospel of Christ bring a truce and peace to our inner turmoil. They can end the fear, conflict and crises caused by the wars that wage within us (Jas 4:1). The war of sinful desires within us (Gal 5:19–21) can be replaced by the fruit of the Spirit (Gal 5:22–23).

God's Sovereignty

Much of our fear and anxiety flows from our failure to understand the sovereignty of God. It was failure to understand this that led Adam and Eve to challenge his sovereignty in the garden of Eden, with predictable results. As Africans would say, "It is sheer madness for an ant to challenge a lion to a fight."

As a result of their foolish challenge, they and all their descendants lost the security, protection and providential care that God provides. No longer did we enjoy security and peace under God's protection. Anxiety and fear rushed in. Without the rule of God, without the protection of God and without the presence of God, we were left with only ourselves and the forces that seek to dominate and ruin our lives.

Our reconciliation with God through the cross of Christ means that we are again under his care. But what does this mean? Why do we still experience anxiety and fear? The answer may be that we do not know enough about God's sovereignty and how it relates to the root sins of anxiety and fear.

God's sovereignty is rooted in his nature as the only self-existing Eternal Being. He is uncreated and has no equal. His unique and transcendent eternal nature guarantees his sovereignty, independence and lordship over all the created universe. He is the foundation for the universal laws to which all creation, including moral beings, are subordinate. He is thus sovereign over all nations, peoples, societies, institutions and social orders. He may delegate some of his power and authority to other lesser moral beings who exercise them on his behalf. But his own sovereignty and lordship cannot be changed or usurped.

True and holy worship, service and obedience to God are rooted in his glorious nature as the Sovereign Lord. His divine sovereignty and lordship command reverence, awe, praise and worship. He is to be worshipped, served and obeyed for his own sake.[75] And he alone is worthy to be worshipped. The Sovereign Lord himself says:

> You shall not make for yourself an image in the form of anything in heaven above or on the earth beneath or in the waters below. You shall not bow down to them or worship them. (Exod 20:4–5)

The basic reason for this prohibition is that idols distort our concept of God, who is spirit (John 4:24) and who must be worshiped in harmony with his nature. Human beings who worship idols are led from dependence on God to reliance on something that expresses their own religious thoughts and motivations.

The Sovereign Lord forbids any form of idolatry or worship of any person or anything, except himself alone (Matt 4:10). When Nebuchadnezzar did not obey this command, he was severely punished for his disobedience (Dan 3–4). Satan, too, refused to accept God's sovereignty and opposed God. But he has been defeated at the cross. God will accept no rival. No one can worship God while also worshipping some other spirit power.

A true understanding of God's sovereignty and lordship over the entire universe is a very powerful antidote to the sins of anxiety and fear – sins which manifest themselves in spiritual idolatry, the worship of a spirit power rather than of God. Worship of our sovereign God leaves no place for worship of lesser beings or nature and also removes our anxiety about our vulnerability, mortality, weakness and insecurity.

Worship of God

But what does it mean to worship God, to give him supreme honour in all our thought and actions? We can learn part of the answer by looking at the words that are translated as "worship" in the Bible.[76] In the Old Testament, the most common word for worship is *sahah*, which means "to bow down," or "to prostrate oneself out of respect". Sometimes, the word *asab*, meaning "to serve", is also translated as "worship". In the New Testament, the word used is *proskuneo*, which means "to make obeisance, do reverence to". This word can be used with reference to God (Matt 4:10; John 4:21–24); human beings (Matt 18:26); demons (Rev 9:20); and idols (Acts 7:43). *Sebomai* means "to revere, stressing the feeling of awe or devotion" and "it is used of worship to God" (Matt 15:9; Acts 16:14; 18:7, 13). *Latreuo* means, "to serve, to render religious service or homage" (Phil 3:3). *Eusebeo* means, "to act piously towards" (Acts 17:23).

True worship has at least three important elements:[77]

- *Reverence.* It is one thing to obey a superior unwillingly; it is another to commit one's thoughts and emotions in that obedience, so that one honours and respects the one obeyed. Jesus said that those who worship God must do so "in spirit and in truth" (John 2:24). The term *spirit* speaks of the personal nature of worship: it is from my person to God's person and involves the intellect, emotions and will. The word *truth* speaks of the content of worship: God is pleased when we worship him, understanding his true character.

- *Public expression*. It was not sufficient to say praises to God privately. We must also give thanks publicly with a thank-offering (Lev 7:12).
- *Service*. Worship and service are often linked in Scripture (Deut 8:19). Furthermore, some of the words used for worship in both the Old and New Testaments originally referred to the labour of slaves for the master. Worship especially includes the joyful service which Christians render to Christ their Master ... an entire life of obedience to God.

Given the time and resources traditional Africans give to worship and religious practices and services, Christianity cannot afford to do less. The heart of the traditional religion is in worship, religious rituals, ceremonies and festivals. But, in most cases, these rituals are not intended to glorify the sovereign God, but, rather, are idolatrous. God is either excluded or included along with many others. Such rituals give only false hope and false security. In response, Christians must stress God's sovereignty, God's providence, the fact that he alone is to be worshipped, and moral and ethical purity and holiness of life.

The Resurrection Power of Jesus

In traditional Africa, people fear spiritual phenomena and dynamic or power phenomena. This fear can be addressed by pointing to the resurrection power of Jesus Christ. We need to stress that his power is superior to all others. Through his death and resurrection, the evil power of Satan, demons and the world, has been broken and dethroned. Satan holds humanity in death, but for believers Jesus has broken Satan's power over death (Heb 2:14, 15; Rev 1:17–18; John 11:25–26; 1 Cor 15; Col 2:15; Eph 1:19–21).

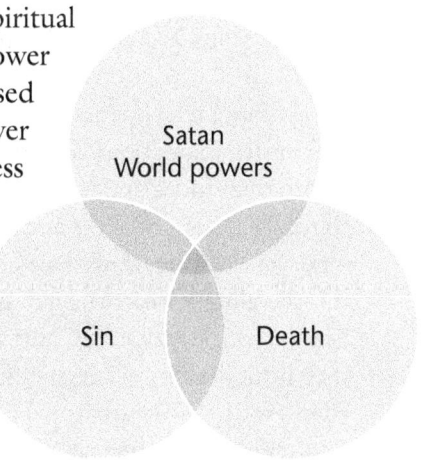

The Cross – Christ's Victory over Death

This resurrection power has placed Christ above all other powers. They are all subject to him and his authority. Thus there is no need to turn to spirit beings and mystical, unseen powers and forces for help, guidance and protection. Jesus has all the power needed to help us. When we apply his resurrection power to daily life, it deals effectively with the issues that cause us anxiety and fear.

Humanity faces four great mysteries that cause anxiety and fear: 1) the mystery of *creation and life;* 2) the mystery of *evil and fate;* 3) the mystery of *sin* and 4) the mystery of *death*.[78] God has a solution to all of them. He has entrusted all mysteries into the hands of his Christ. And the one who puts his faith in Christ has the one who has power and authority over all the mysteries of life and creation. Jesus Christ has the answer to spirit powers that dominate the world.

Jesus' Teachings on Worry

We are often anxious about whether we will be able to find or keep the basic necessities: life, food, shelter and clothing. There are many things that threaten to take these away from us, including illness, unemployment, riots and wars. When such worries strike, we need to turn to what Jesus had to say on this subject.

> Therefore I tell you, do not worry about your life, what you will eat or drink; or about your body, what you will wear. Is not life more than food, and the body more than clothes? Look at the birds of the air; they do not sow or reap or store away in barns, and yet your heavenly Father feeds them. Are you not much more valuable than they? Can any of you by worrying add a single hour to your life? And why do you worry about clothes? See how the flowers of the field grow. They do not labour or spin. Yet I tell you that not even Solomon in all his splendour was dressed like one of these. If that is how God clothes the grass of the field, which is here today and tomorrow is thrown into the fire, will he not much more clothe you – you of little faith? So do not worry, saying, "What shall we eat?" or "What shall we drink?" or "What shall we wear?" For the pagans run

after these things, and your heavenly Father knows that you need them. But seek first his kingdom and his righteousness, and all these things will be given to you as well. Therefore do not worry about tomorrow, for tomorrow will worry about itself. Each day has enough trouble of its own. (Matt 6:25–34)

Paul was applying this truth when the told the Philippians

Do not be anxious about anything, but in every situation, by prayer and petition, with thanksgiving, present your requests to God. And the peace of God, which transcends all understanding, will guard your hearts and your minds in Christ Jesus. (Phil 4:6–7)

Instead of being consumed with worry, they were to rejoice in the Lord and devote their mental energy to thinking about things that were "excellent or praiseworthy" and to following the truth of the gospel (Phil 4:4, 8–9).

Summary

When God is absent, our lives are full of anxiety and fear, characterized by broken relationships and alienation from God, others, nature and even ourselves. To be able to live peacefully we must turn to God and live under his sovereignty, worshipping, serving and living in loyalty to him. Such a relationship is made possible by Christ's work on the cross in which he bore the penalty for our sin and now makes those who trust in him acceptable to God. As we develop a true fear of and reverence for God, our tendency to idolatry, anxiety and fear will be driven out. We will be able to live as those called to believe and trust God, to depend upon him and to live under his sovereignty and providence. We will indeed be able to say, "If God is for us, who can be against us?" (Rom 8:31).

PART IV: SIN ISSUES IN MODERN AFRICA

This final part of the book deals with some issues that are particularly relevant to modern Africa – although they may also manifest themselves in other ways in other parts of the world.

The first issue to be addressed is spiritual idolatry, which is the manifestation of spirit power in the lives of modern Africans, whether Christians, Muslims or modernists. Many Africans have come to Christ without having their minds renewed and transformed by the gospel of Christ. Thus they are still influenced by traditional beliefs and practices regarding spirit power. Their religion involves accommodation, adaptation or syncretism. Christ's power must break down the dominant traditional spirit power if there is to be true conversion and transformation.

The second important issue that we need to address is the persistence of communal and social sins. Human crises, tribal wars, conflict and violence in Africa stem from spiritual alienation and broken relationships. Personal Christian conversion that does not affect this area of life leaves the African church very weak and powerless to change and transform the continent. Devastating communal and social sins wreak the havoc we are already witnessing.

16

SPIRITUAL IDOLATRY IN MODERN AFRICA

There is a saying: "In everything, an African is religious." But just because religion and spirituality dominate the life of an African, one cannot assume that he or she is free of the sin of spiritual idolatry. In fact, their religiosity or spirituality may be an impetus to spiritual idolatry. Excessive spirituality can become a breeding ground for sins of this nature.

African Traditional Religion endures because it has spirit power behind it. Colonialism, Western missionary Christianity and Islam may have destroyed its shrines, blood sacrifices and institutions, yet it lives on in the minds and traditions of many Africans. Even second-generation Christians who know little about traditional religion still live under its power. As a world view it does not need any physical institution to sustain it. In fact, it thrives in churches, mosques and Western institutions.

We see the influence of this world view when African Christians express beliefs or act in ways that reflect the traditional beliefs that were described in chapter two. Many African churches with no depth of theology feel free to experiment with beliefs, rituals and practices that may look innocent but eventually tend towards neopaganism and syncretism. The words or acts may sound familiar, but they can be infused with a new meaning, which may be very different from biblical teaching. This confusion is one reason why many attempts to deal with spiritual idolatry in modern Africa are ineffective.

Western neopaganism has also great influence in modern Africa and is increasingly becoming presented as another "new gospel". It manifests itself in religious cults whose practices are at variance with sound biblical teaching.

An African Ancestor in the Garden of Eden

Let me retell the story of Adam and Eve from an African perspective, imagining what would have happened if God had put one of our African ancestors in the garden of Eden.

Our African ancestor would have been given similar instructions to that given to Adam and Eve in Genesis 3. However, instead of being forbidden to eat of the Tree of the Knowledge of Good and Evil, he would have been forbidden to eat of the Tree of the Knowledge of Spirit and Power. The temptation offered to him would have included the promises, "You will not die" and "Your eyes will be opened and you will be like God, *knowing spirit and power*". Those are things that would tempt an African! We lust after spirit and power, rather than the knowledge of good and evil. This hungering for spiritualism and dynamism (power) apart from God is the root of our spiritual idolatry. It lures traditionalists away from the worship of the Creator God. African scholars may say that these spiritual powers are intermediaries comparable to Christ, but the Bible clearly teaches that worshipping such powers is a fall from true worship of God.

The most grievous sin we can commit against God is spiritual idolatry, the failure to worship him alone. In fact, the Bible compares idolatry to adultery. In worship, the worshipper and the thing worshipped become, as it were, one flesh, just as a man and his wife do when they have sexual intercourse. It is a communion of deep relationship that is sealed spiritually in the giving of oneself completely to another. To take the worship that is due to God and offer it to some other being is like a husband or wife having sexual intercourse with someone else.

Western Neopagan Spirituality

In the eighteenth and nineteenth centuries Western missionaries came to Africa with the gospel of Jesus Christ. Africans embraced Christianity and abandoned their pagan religions and practices. Today, African Christians see Westerners abandoning their Christianity. The rise of secularism, pluralism, relativism and postmodernism has dethroned Western ethnocentrism and Christianity, and created a religious vacuum.

Some are seeking to fill this vacuum by reviving the pagan gods their forefathers had abandoned.

One result of this swing to neopaganism is that these days many prefer the heretical writings from the days of the early church to the Bible. In the eyes of some, the *Gospel of St. Thomas* outranks the Gospel of John. Gnostic literature is revered more than that of the apostles and early church fathers. Popular books like *The Da Vinci Code* attempt to discredit Christianity, Jesus, the apostles and the church.

This new religion in the West is quite different from African traditional religions and older animism or paganism. It merely uses pagan religious symbolism and spirituality to frame its reaction against Western culture and Christianity. It is a modern religion born of Western secularism, religious pluralism, cultural relativism and postmodernism. It is inherently humanistic, based upon a strong emphasis on individualism and human freedom. It is a critique of the Western scientific and technological enterprise, its materialism, rationalism, and hedonism. Unfortunately, the Christian approach to life is also included in this critique. It is a return to simplistic humanism, self-intuition or insight, and the ancient folkloric tales of pre-Christian Europe and North America. Much of it is self-worship and nature worship. Western neopaganism also borrows freely from the spirituality of Eastern religions and animism to create an alternative spirituality in protest against Western secularist culture and the Christian faith and traditions. The Christian God is often claimed to be an authoritarian or a male chauvinist while Neopaganism and the New Age religions are held up as the new spiritual and cultural liberators of the West. They give people the liberty to worship the free spirit of man, ancient folklore and nature without any restraints or social guidelines. They are, in fact, a search for inner peace and harmony with nature. This is a new spiritual idolatry that worships nature and humanity.

Neopagan spirituality has the following key elements:[79]

- *Animism*, or the view that Nature (always capitalized) is sacred and that all things are imbued with a certain vitality, "divine spark" or life force.
- *Pantheism*, or the view that divinity is inseparable from Nature and is immanent in Nature.

- *Polytheism*, or the view that reality is multiple and diverse. There is a spirit of radical inclusivity which stands in direct contrast to the exclusivity of orthodox Christianity, Judaism, and Islam.
- *Subjectivity*, or the view that spirituality is to be based on your own subjective experience and personal vision rather than on objective dogma or written creeds.
- *Reintegration*, or the view that the goal of spirituality is to relink or reconnect the self with Nature. There is a strong element of "holism" in Neopaganism – everything is related. There is no distinction between spiritual and material, sacred and secular.
- *Self-Divinization*, the view that we are all gods.

This Western form of spiritual idolatry has made inroads into modern Africa and influenced Africa's own forms of neopaganism, cultism and syncretism.

Idolatry

The African concept of spirit power, which was discussed at length in chapter 2, and the above description of Western neopaganism give us a good understanding of the nature of spiritual idolatry in our modern times.

In the last chapter, we defined idolatry within the context of God's sovereignty. There we saw it as an expression of anxiety and fear. It is religious activity in the absence of God. It is also a form of worship that excludes God or merely includes him among others.

The sins that arise from spiritual idolatry are not like the sins of human nature which we examined in the previous chapters. These sins affect our fundamental relationship with God as the Creator and Redeemer, and our worship of God. It is worth looking at what the Bible has to say about idolatry.

First of all, how does it describe it? In the New Testament, the Greek word used is *eidolon*, which means: "a phantom or likeness"; "an idea or fancy"; "an image to represent a false god"; "the false god worshipped in an image" (Acts 7:41; 1 Cor 12:1; Rev 9:20; Acts 15:20; Rom 2:22; 1 Cor 8:4, 7; 10:19; 2 Cor 6:16).[80] In the Old Testament, many Hebrew words are used to describe idols.[81]

- *awen* means "nought, vanity, iniquity and wickedness" (Isa 66:3);
- *shiqqu* means "filth and impurity-immoral rites associated with idolatry, ceremonial uncleanness" (Ezek 37:23; Nah 3:6);
- *gillulim* means "droppings of dung" (Ezek 6:4–6, 9, 13);
- *bosheth* means "a shameful thing, filthy and immoral worship associated with Baal worship";
- *elil* means "a thing of nought, something that does not exist" (1 Chr 16:16; Ps 96:5; 97:7).

These words express God's hostility to anything that replaces him at the centre of life.

Idolatry is man's substituted worship of the *creature* in place of God (Rom 1:18–32). Whatever becomes a substitute for God, becomes an idol. And whatever beliefs or practices are associated with that are in themselves idolatrous. Thus there is idolatry in the African quest for spirits and mystical powers and forces from gods, divinities, spirit beings, and any form of religious practices and worship not directed to God alone. Such a search for the aid of spirit beings shows that we are not recognizing the truth that God is our provider, sustainer and protector and the only one whom we should worship.

Steyne provides a list of some of traditional practices that are prohibited in the Bible as idolatrous, but are practiced within human societies.[82] (Although even in traditional African societies, some of these practices were prohibited as abominations.) As you read through the list, note that what is important is not the prohibition itself but the theological reason for the prohibition. All the practices listed in the table involved dealings with spirits and demonic powers other than God. Our God is a Sovereign Lord and will not tolerate any rival. He demands our absolute loyalty (Exod 20:2–6; Isa 42).

Witchcraft and sorcery	Deut 18:9–14; 2 Chr 33:6; 2 Kgs 9:22; Micah 5:12, 15; Nahum 3:1, 4–7; Gal 5:19–21; Exod 22:18
Contact with ancestors	Isa 8:19, 22; 19:23; 1 Sam 28:7–12; Deut 18:11; Lev 20:27
Shamanism	Isa 2:6; 47:13; Deut 18:11, 14; Gen 41:8; Acts 13:6, 8; Jer 14:14; Exod 22:18; Lev 19:31; 20:6, 27

Divination	Deut 18:9–10, 18, 20, 22; 1 Sam 15:23; Ezek 13:6, 9, 23; 21:21–22, 29, 32; Acts 16:16; Isa 47:13, 14; Num 23:23; 2 Kgs 17:17; Jer 14:14
Rituals	Isa 1:11–20; Deut 5:29; Ezek 14:3–11
Charms	Jer 8:17; Ezek 11:21
Fire walking and human sacrifice	Lev 18:21; 20:1–5; Deut 12:29–31; 18:10; 2 Kgs 16:3; 17:17; 23:13; Jer 19:4–5; 32:35; 49:1, 3; Ezek 16:21
Spells and curses	Josh 13:22; Num 22:6; Isa 47:9, 12
Propitious times	Lev 19:26; Deut 18:10, 14; 2 Kgs 21:6; 2 Chr 33:6
Magical practices	Acts 13:10
Demonic powers	1 Peter 5:8; Eph 6:12; Jude 6; Mark 1:23, 24; 5:2, 3, 5, 8, 9, 13; Matt 8:29; 9:32, 33; 12:24, 43–45; Rev 16:14; Luke 8:2; James 2:19; 1 Tim 4:1; Judges 9:23; 2 Peter 2:4
Animal spirits	Lev 17:7; Deut 32:16, 17
Body mutilation and tattoos	Lev 19:28; Deut 14:1
Spirit protectors	Lev 26:1
Signs	Num 24:1; Deut 4:19; 13:1–3
Prostitution and fertility rites	Deut 23:17
Sacrifices and libations	Deut 32:37–38
Power objects and/or fetishes	1 Sam 4:3

Regarding this unique status of our God in relationship to worship and idolatry, Adeyemo states:

> In the New Testament, both Jesus Christ and the apostles taught and demonstrated that only God is to be worshipped. Any attempt to worship anyone else besides the triune God is a perversion of truth. This is Satan's effort to secure for himself what belongs properly to God alone (Matt 4:9) ... Undue deference paid to men borders at times on worship and this is resisted by the disciples (Acts 10:25, 26; 14:11–14) ... Explicit commands are given in the Bible not to worship any other, be it a celestial body, natural phenomena, or ancestors, except the living God (Exod 20:3; Deut 4:14–20; Job 31:24–28; Col 2:18). In the light of this sharp distinction, this writer understands worship in the traditional religion as idolatry with

the best commentary in Romans 1:21–25 and 1 Corinthians 8:1–7.[83]

It is important to take note of this, for prosperity and peace are related to keeping God's laws and worshipping him alone:

> I command you today to love the Lord your God, to walk in obedience to him, and to keep his commands, decrees and laws; then you will live and increase, and the Lord your God will bless you in the land you are entering to possess. But if your heart turns away and you are not obedient, and if you are drawn away to bow down to other gods and worship them, I declare to you this day that you will certainly be destroyed. You will not live long in the land you are crossing the Jordan to enter and possess. This day I call the heavens and the earth as witnesses against you that I have set before you life and death, blessings and curses. Now choose life, so that you and your children may live. (Deut 30:16–19)

Syncretism

One of the ways in which error creeps into the church is through syncretism, which changes the meaning of a belief, a symbol or a ritual so that it is no longer in accord with the true meaning of the gospel or the Bible. The effect is to move worshippers who accept this syncretism into spiritual idolatry.

Syncretism can be defined as

> the process by which elements of one religion are assimilated into another religion resulting in a change in the fundamental tenets or nature of those religions. It is the union of two or more opposite beliefs, so that the synthesized form is a new thing. It is not always a total fusion, but may be a combination of separate segments that remain identifiable compartments ... Syncretism of the Christian gospel occurs when critical or basic elements of the gospel are replaced by religious elements from the host culture. It often results from a tendency or attempt

to undermine the uniqueness of the gospel as found in the Scriptures or the incarnate Son of God.[84]

It is important not to confuse syncretism with what is called the theology of incarnation or inculturation. Inculturation is a positive thing, intended to deepen understanding and meaning by use of the indigenous language or symbols. It does not distort the truth. Syncretism, however, distorts or changes the meaning entirely.

Syncretism can also give rise to religious cults, that is, new religious movements or institutions that combine elements of various older religious traditions.

Examples of Modern Spiritual Idolatry in Africa

Christians who practice spiritual idolatry may hold to the following fundamental traditional beliefs or practices in addition to their Christianity.

- *They may seek to control, conciliate, acquire and use spiritual and mystical powers and forces to meet their personal, or communal needs and purposes.*

  Some Christians look for spirit powers that can be used to meet their or their communities' needs. They may want to control a situation or their circumstance, or to pacify or appease themselves or others. If the spirit powers involved are not sanctioned by God or the Bible, this represents a slide into spiritual idolatry. Some Christians get involved in these spiritual activities out of ignorance and lack of spiritual discernment. We need to remind them of the Apostle John's words:

  > Dear friends, do not believe every spirit, but test the spirits to see whether they are from God, because many false prophets have gone out into the world. This is how you can recognize the Spirit of God: Every spirit that acknowledges that Jesus Christ has come in the flesh is from God, but every spirit that does not acknowledge Jesus is not from God. This is the spirit

of the antichrist, which you have heard is coming and even now is already in the world. (1 John 4:1–4)

- *They may develop rituals and ceremonies as means of controlling, conciliating and acquiring spiritual and mystical powers and forces.*
  Some Christians become involved in rituals or ceremonies designated as sure means of realizing desired goals. They perform certain rituals or ceremonies that involve spirit powers not sanctioned by God or the Bible. When one encounters this type of situation, it is important to look for elements of spirit power that are not Christ-power or of the Holy Spirit. Spiritual discernment is necessary, for spirits can imitate Christ-power and the power of the Holy Spirit.

- *They may develop mystical means of exercising control over the spirit world.*
  Some people have mystical, psychic or spiritual powers that enable them to see visions, have revelations, perform healings and miracles, speak in tongues, and so on. Some naïve people think that anyone who has these gifts must be a very good Christian. But these works of spirit power are not a criterion for determining who is a good Christian. The Bible makes it clear that other spirits can imitate certain things that the Holy Spirit does. In Egypt and Babylon, as recorded in Genesis and Daniel, magicians, astrologers, enchanters and diviners could perform signs and wonders, but these were not sanctioned by God. Those with discernment should look for the source of these people's power. Is it from God and his Holy Spirit or from some other spirit being? Jesus warned us,

> Not everyone who says to me, "Lord, Lord," will enter the kingdom of heaven, but only the one who does the will of my Father who is in heaven. Many will say to me on that day, "Lord, Lord, did we not prophesy in your name, and in your name drive out demons and perform many miracles?" Then I will tell them plainly, "I never knew you. Away from me, you evildoers!" (Matt 7:21–23)

- *They may develop mystical means of communicating with the spirit world.*

  Many people desire to communicate with spirits, whether the spirits of their ancestors, demons or other spirits. Some want to know the future or what is going to happen to them. Some seek for spiritual guidance. Many people talk about their communication with God, Jesus or the Holy Spirit, but this is not enough to prove that such communication comes from the true and living God. Spirit beings can be imitators. Discernment is needed to identify the source of this spiritual means of communication and guidance.

- *They may consult spiritual specialists.*

  Many people think that they have limited abilities when it comes to spiritual matters and so rely on spiritual specialists. They go to consult those who are said to possess spiritual powers beyond the ordinary. Some seek spiritual help by visiting prayer houses, shrines, caves, mountains, rivers, forests, graveyards, or certain important locations. Some of those seeking prayer or spiritual help are misled into demonic and spiritist practices. Some spiritual specialists add certain teachings to the word of God or have some elaborate rituals to go along with their teachings. What we need to identify is the source of powers that a spiritual specialist has. Who are they consulting or turning to? There are some who begin with God, Jesus Christ, the Holy Spirit or the word of God, but move on into strange teachings or practices. They are merely using the name of Jesus, God, the Holy Spirit or the Bible to lure their clients into deeper spiritism.

  African Christians who follow any of the above practices may be maintaining traditional beliefs, engaging with a religious cult, or allowing religious syncretism in their thinking. Not every form of Christianity in Africa is true to biblical and Christian teachings. For this reason, we need spiritual discernment.

Quest for spiritual and mystical power

African spirituality, whether traditional or Christian or modern, always has a strong element of the quest for spiritual and mystical powers to deliver solutions to problems. This power may be sought from God; from lesser beings, gods or divinities; from spiritual and mystical powers and forces; or from some combination of these. It is thus important that we ask the question, "Who is it who grants or answers prayers?" If the response is that the saints or ancestors or spirits answer prayers, then they have centres of spiritual powers and objects of worship. Saints or ancestors who answer prayers have become entities that have usurped the place of God, and dealing with such is spiritual idolatry.

Quest for life force and spiritual powers

In modern Africa, the quest for spirituality has not diminished but has grown increasingly popular. Traditionalists, Christians and modernists all exhibit some forms of spirituality and religion. Christianity has to define the distinctive nature of its spirituality as different from other forms of spirituality.

Traditional Africa believes that life force is found in everything, especially in animal life and nature. The acquisition or possession of life force or spirit power adds strength, power or success to a human being. The one who possesses it can rise above the ordinary, do extraordinary things and receive extra protection or guidance. This added power makes for a greater sense of security and allays some fears and anxieties. It is believed that life force or spirit power can be obtained in the following ways:

- Through the senses by means of drugs, severe discipline, self-emptying, the discipline of silence, fasting, dancing and the power of music.

- Through the ancestors by association with their lineage, especially if it includes powerful heroes, leaders and warriors. Association with ancestors takes various forms including reverence, respect and worship of the ancestors as guardians of the family or community; contact with and use of the sacred objects known to have been used and kept by the ancestors; and consulting or speaking to the spirits of the ancestors. Christians involved in these traditional practices are actually practising idolatry as these practices are contrary to biblical teaching.

- Through regular participation in religious celebrations, liturgies and rituals. Spiritual and mystical powers have the tendency to decrease or be lost altogether if one is not always in touch with their source. Through regular participation in religious celebrations, liturgies and rituals, one can enhance or maintain spirit power. Some of these spiritual practices may appear to be harmless, but when they are contrary to biblical teachings, they are forms of spiritual idolatry.

- Through sacrifices and the use of blood, the burial of animals and sometimes even of human beings in strategic places. A strong belief in the potency of sacrifice or blood drives people to all forms of sacrifices and rituals so as to acquire life force and spiritual powers.
- Through the use of charms, sacred objects, weapons and other paraphernalia. It is believed that certain objects have a life force. This force can be transferred to other objects through rituals, and then charms and amulets can be used to protect oneself or bring harm to others. The rituals may sometimes even claim to be Christian. However, before being accepted as such they must pass the test of Scripture and be sanctioned by the believing Christian community.

All Africans attach a very high social and religious value to rituals and ceremonies as means of acquiring life force and spiritual powers. Rituals also serve to maintain or restore harmony between human beings and the spirit world, and are a means of communication with the spirit world. It is through rituals that specialists acquire the knowledge, skills and spiritual and mystical powers associated with their professional roles. Given the importance of ceremonies and rituals, it is very important that Christians have biblical guidelines in these areas. Even rituals that claim to be Christian must be examined for traces of traditional religion and syncretism. It is quite possible that some Christians engage in certain rituals or ceremonies without being aware of the spiritual powers involved or recognizing that seeking to acquire life force or spirit powers is a form of spiritual idolatry.

Quest to control the spirit world

Power-consciousness and spirit beings dominate African traditional beliefs, practices and rituals, and the desire to be able to exercise control in the spirit world is still very strong among religious Africans, whether traditionalists, Christians or modernists. The most common means of exercising such control are incantations, symbolism, witchcraft, sorcery, charms, fetishes, and white and black magic.

Quest to communicate with the spirit world

There is great interest in communicating with the spirit world through divination in order to find out about one's future, destiny, and well-being and what may happen to one's family, clan or tribe. Divination can also be used to gain access to the source of mystical and spiritual powers that can be tapped to meet one's needs. It can reveal how to protect oneself from the evil activities of witches, wizards and mediums and from the wicked and dreadful unseen and unpredictable mystical and spirit powers. Armed with knowledge acquired by divination, one has power, confidence, assurance and boldness to face the challenges of life and triumph over them through esoteric and mystical means. One can overcome human limitations, finitude, impotence and dependence and be able to receive and interpret messages from the spirit world for both personal and communal well-being and to maintain harmony between human beings and the spirits or gods.

Divination has a long history, and many different types of divination are mentioned in the Bible. These include rhabdomancy (throwing sticks in the air and examining their position when they fall – Ezek 21:21); hepatoscopy (examining the entrails of an animal – Ezek 21:21); teraphim (images of dead ancestors, possibly used in spiritualism – Ezek 21:21); necromancy (consulting the dead – Lev 19:31); astrology (drawing conclusions from the relative positions of planets – Isa 47:13); and hydromancy (observing pictures in water – Gen 44:5).[85]

Those who practice divination in the Bible include astrologers (Isa 47:13), diviners (Deut 18:14), false prophets (Jer 14:14), magicians (Gen 41:8), mediums (Deut 18:11), necromancers (Deut 18:11), sorcerers (Exod 22:18; Acts 13:6 and spiritists (Deut 18:11).

The Bible is strongly opposed to all divination. This is not only because it is often fraudulent (Ezek 13:6–7) but also because divination is "a pagan counterpart of prophecy. Divination is by demonic power, whereas genuine prophecy is by the Spirit of God. God, therefore, detests divination of any kind".[86] That is why it is described as an abomination (Deut 18:11–12) and is punishable by death (Lev 20:6, 27). So are other occult practices like magic, sorcery and witchcraft (Exod 22:18; Lev 19:26; 20:27; Deut 18:10–12; Rev 21:8).

Yet another reason for the Bible's opposition to practices like divination and witchcraft is that

> they are a denial of faith. True believers walk humbly with their God, accepting that, no matter what the circumstances; God is still in control of their affairs. Having been saved by faith, they now live by faith (Gal 2:20; Eph 4:17–24; Col 1:11–13; Heb 11:6). Jesus Christ has triumphed over all the unseen powers of evil and through him believers too can triumph (Eph 1:19–21; 2:6; Col 2:8–10; 3:1–3).[87]

Quest to maintain harmony with the spirit world

African Traditional Religion attaches great importance to reciprocal communication between human beings and the spirit world. This communication is regarded as necessary in order to maintain harmony or balance between the human world and the spirit world. This harmony is always under siege, and so it is important to stay informed on whether one is in a favourable standing before the gods. If not, what has gone wrong? And how can things be set right? Communication is necessary to maintain relations between the gods or spirits and humanity.

Traditional Africans do not only busy themselves with what they can get from the gods and the spirits, but also with what they can give in return so as to enhance fellowship, communion and reciprocity between themselves and the gods. The gods and spirits make demands on their human clients. Sometimes these demands are communicated by the gods and spirits and sometimes they are assumed by the human worshipper. What is needed are often sacrifices and offerings that will repair relationships and restore the longed-for harmony. African Christians too may be tempted to make sacrifices or to present offerings or gifts to appease the gods or ancestors and so avert evil or calamity.

Parallels can be drawn between some of the traditional African sacrifices and some of those mandated in the Pentateuch, the first five books of the Old Testament. However, it is important to note that the Jewish sacrifices were intended to replace, not imitate, those of the religions around them. Moreover, they were offered only to God, and not to subordinate spirits or ancestors.

The Old Testament system of sacrifices was set aside by the atoning sacrifice of Jesus Christ on the cross, which eliminated all need for further sacrifices (Heb 8:13; 10:1–18). He is the true Passover Lamb that the Old Testament sacrifice foreshadowed, the sacrificial Lamb of God who takes away sin (John 1:29, 36; 1 Cor 5:7–8; 1 Pet 1:18–19). He is our sin offering (Rom 8:3) and the guilt-offering, the suffering Servant of Isaiah 53 (1 John 1:7–9). His sacrifice is one of the chief themes of the whole New Testament.

The only sacrifices that are still required in the New Testament are spiritual sacrifices offered in response to God's love and mercy (1 Pet 2:5). They are to offer themselves to God as living sacrifices (Rom 12:1; 2 Cor 8:5) and will then be able to offer God acceptable sacrifices of worship, praise and service (Rom 15:16; Phil 4:18; Heb 13:15).

The other way traditional religion maintained harmony between nature, spiritual beings and humanity was by observing religious festivals and sacred days. Thus Africans would celebrate new moons and the beginning of the rainy or planting season, the harvest season, the new yams festivals and the hunting season. The Jews too observed similar festivals. Some of the traditional festivals have been transformed into Christian festivals. But African Christians who participate in such feasts and ceremonies need to be sure that they have been sanctioned by the believing Christian community in order to avoid participating in what may be an idolatrous cult.

Observance of taboos

Taboos govern numerous aspects of Africa's social, cultural and religious life. They set out the codes of conduct or the do's and don'ts of a given community. They thus function as sacred moral codes that prescribe the behaviour required to maintain cosmic or communal harmony. They are tools for socio-cultural and religious conditioning, maintaining the social order and harmony and structures of meanings and world views.

Christians in Africa have to take care to ensure that the sources of their moral, ethical and social behaviour and practice are rooted in the Bible if their morality and ethics are not to be confused and less than biblical.

Consultation of African Specialists

The complexity of African traditional beliefs and practices in relationship to the spirit world, has given rise to what we may call African specialists. People turn to shamans, witchdoctors, prophets, priests, mediums and medicine men or women for professional help in negotiating with the spirit world. These specialists are believed to have extraordinary skills and powers to deal with problems and to have insight into secrets and mysteries. They are thus qualified to stand between ordinary people and the gods or spirits.

The esteem accorded to these religious professionals has transferred into contemporary Christianity in Africa. Someone who is known as a "man of God" is highly regarded. This can lead to abuses and the establishment of cults. African Christians should be discouraged from consulting any religious specialist who is not a genuine Christian. Discernment is needed to detect traces of syncretistic beliefs.

Joining secret cults

Secret cults play a major role in African traditional religions, for Africans are acutely aware of the mysteries of life. The secret cults offer initiates access to knowledge that goes beyond common knowledge and common sense.

African Christians may join these secret societies. Some of them are cults, which offer initiates deeper knowledge of Jesus Christ which goes beyond what is taught in the Bible. They thus appeal to human curiosity and the quest for deeper knowledge. But the Bible makes it clear that it contains all that we need to know about Jesus Christ (1 Cor 1:18–2:5; Col 1:15–20; Heb 1:1–13). He is the full revelation of God, and there is no secret revelation that goes beyond what is presented by the prophets and apostles and the gospels.

Spiritual Powers and Warfare

In their comparative study of traditional religion and Christianity, most African scholars have ignored the significance of the spiritual powers and forces in traditional religion and culture. But ever since its arrival in

Africa, Christianity has been engaged in spiritual warfare with the spirit powers and forces that lie behind traditional religion. Stories abound about how early missionaries and early converts were attacked by demonic forces but overcame them by Christ's power. They confronted the spirit powers of the traditional religion face to face.

The same struggle continues today as we witness how traditional spirituality and power-consciousness are still shaping and moulding African religious thought. It is giving rise to neopaganism, religious cults and religious syncretism. It also complicates Christians' understanding of sin and its solution.

Many Christians are drawn into cults or sects that show the outward forms of Christian spirituality while underneath is the bed-rock of pagan spirituality. They manifest spirit powers, working miracles, performing healings, speaking in tongues, and showing signs and wonders that could be mistaken for the work of the Holy Spirit. Such counterfeit spirituality is both seductive and destructive. It is thus very important that we develop guidelines like those set out in this chapter for identifying the manifestations of spiritual idolatry in modern Africa. We also need to clear up the many misunderstandings regarding the nature, attributes and character of the triune God and God's solution to the problem of sin as outlined in the Bible.

17

SOCIAL AND COMMUNAL SINS IN AFRICA

Despite the very high percentage of Christians in many African countries, our societies are rife with crises, conflict and violence. Poverty, scarce resources and a lack of social mobility are all feeding into a dramatic increase in social and communal sins. Many of the perpetrators of the Rwandan genocide of 1994 claimed to be Christians. Clearly it is not enough to focus only on the sin of individuals while ignoring the power of social and communal sins that are rooted in kinship and communal values.

Foundations of Attitudes, Behaviour and Social Practice

Social and communal sins are rooted in beliefs, attitudes, behaviour and practices that spring from African Traditional Religion and its encounter with Christianity and modernity. This encounter has generated new social formations and values that complicate the network of relationships among individuals, people groups, communities, societies, institutions and nation-states. However, before looking at these we need to review the five basic traditional beliefs that influence ethics and morality in traditional Africa:

- *The pursuit of cosmic harmony*, which springs from an organic or holistic view of life.

- *The pursuit of spiritual meaning*, which springs from the view that all of life is spiritual and that events must be interpreted from a spiritual perspective.
- *The pursuit of mystical and supernatural powers*, which springs from the dynamism that pervades traditional thinking and spurs a desire to obtain power.
- *The importance of a kinship community*, which springs from a communal view of life.
- *Fatalism*, which springs from a belief that one is powerless in the face of overwhelming spiritual forces, so that the difficulties of life must be accepted.

In the complex modern environment in Africa, these values lead to an ethic which accepts that the end justifies the means. Individuals and communities focus on achieving goals for themselves, regardless of the consequences for others. The result is social and communal sins that reflect the dominant concerns of a particular individual, community, society, tribe, institution or nation.

The belief that the pursuit of moral goals takes precedence over moral behaviour undermines responsible behaviour and ethics. It means that individuals in one community or tribe have no need to show consideration and respect to those of others outside their own group. Similarly, the collective of a community or a tribe need not show consideration and respect for another community or tribe. When groups with this way of thinking and set of values are brought into close contact, their behaviour in pursuit of their divergent moral interests can easily ignite conflict, leading to crises and violence.

The importance of kinship in Africa means that for many Africans responsibility to one's blood relations takes precedence over any obligations to strangers and outsiders. This attitude is the bane of African nations since it fosters tribalism, sectionalism and denominationalism. It results in behaviour that breeds crises, conflict, violence, a domineering spirit, prejudice and stereotyping. Communities are alienated from one another. The effects of kinship values are seen in institutions and even Christian denominations that are dominated by people from certain ethnic groups or classes.

The focus on the community rather than the individual also means that communal moral accountability counts far more than personal accountability. Personal responsibility is undermined. An individual's attitude and behaviour are judged as good or bad solely by whether they are in accord with group or tribal values, regardless of how they would be seen in terms of universal, national or institutional values. Some churches and states become ungovernable because communal or kinship values hold them to ransom.

Attitudes, behaviour, ethics and morality are dominated by fear of those with moral power. Thus, for example, fear of how the tribe or community will respond influences the way individuals behave and the way issues are resolved. The resulting ethics is based on the principle that "might is right", which undermines justice, equality and freedom. The weak are ignored; the strong are feared. We see the results in the insecurity, instability, crises, violence and chaos that flow from the exercise of the rule of fear by dictators and the powerful.

In societies where poverty reigns and resources are few, people tend to pursue the good life or security at the expense of good moral behaviour or ethics. An insecure environment and a corrupt society, in combination with conflict and mistrust between individuals and groups, contributes to the rise of a new form of ethics, attitudes and behaviour that is neither traditionally African nor Western. Thus an African leader may steal billions of dollars from his poor nation and lodge them in a Western bank. Traditional African kinship values do not sanction such behaviour, nor does Western ethics. And yet it is done with impunity in Africa. This is a result of a broken spiritual relationship or alienation. The thief is alienated from his traditional society and all its values and also from a modern society and all its values. As a pragmatist, he uses his modern context to formulate a new value that is neither African nor Western.

When guilt and shame, right and wrong, responsibility and accountability are defined solely within the context of communal or kinship values, those who loot the government, companies or institutions for the benefit of their own group think of themselves as heroes. They are not ashamed of what they have done, but proud of it. Their communities encourage such behaviour by rewarding them with honorific titles and social recognition. Outsiders may condemn them, but they are hailed by insiders. Such morality encourages corruption and the dominance of one group over others within African states.

If we are to address these issues, we need to recognize that people's attitudes and behaviour are influenced both by their innate fallen human nature and by the culture in which they were raised. And this is very difficult to change. We all have specific ways of seeing, understanding and interpreting the world around us, and we apply our moral codes in different ways. There is ample scope for conflict, misunderstanding and problems. This is even more the case because human culture and religion are fallen and sinful, and hence they generate spirit powers that lead to communal and social sins. Humanity without God developed its culture, religion, ethics and morality in brokenness and alienation. Whenever humanity comes together, it is ridden with anxiety and fear of others. And so we respond in anxiety and fear, leading to conflict and violence.

Kinship and Communal Morality

Of all moral laws, the law of kinship is the most powerful and pervasive in traditional Africa. It is the queen of African moral laws. It determines and creates two types of morality and ethics: 1) a code of morality and ethics for insiders who share a common ancestor (the blood-group, the community, the tribe) and 2) another code of morality and ethics for outsiders (strangers).

Outsiders are usually treated as those outside of the commonwealth. They may or may not be accorded human status. They may or may not be treated better than animals. They are not entitled to 1) equal treatment; 2) ownership; 3) affinity, loyalty and obligations; 4) community rights and protection.

The moral norm is that "blood is thicker than water": what is of your blood-group is yours and takes precedence over what is not of your blood-group; the interests of your blood group outweigh self-interest and altruism; you should take care of your blood-group first before considering outsiders.

In a kinship system, the place of individuals is as well defined as that of an outsider. The individual does not exist for him- or herself and has no individual social life. Nor does the individual determine his or her own course of life, as in Western individualism. One's life and entire existence is built on the foundation of kinship. Individualism for its own sake is not a moral norm, but an aberration.

Individuals in modern African states are usually under the grip of kinship, tribal and racial values and ethics. Their quest for tribal or racial control of state power or modern institutions has often led to tensions, conflict and sometimes violence. Cases abound where ethnic groups demand that their sons and daughters comply with the wishes and the interests of their blood-group and blood-community rather than with universal and national values.

Traditional religion, morality and ethics are also rooted in a blood relationship with ones' ancestors. They do not derive from an external, objective and transcendent source. Values and ethics are communal, local and private, not universal. Thus they do not apply to the whole world. The moral laws derived from the cosmos, the spirit world, the gods and the divinities are therefore limited in their scope and application. They are to be interpreted in terms of communitarian values. Other kinship communities are governed by their own set of moral laws. They may be similar or different, but have their own authority and legitimacy. The overriding ethical principle is relativism, not universalism.

Modern national constitutions with their ethical and moral codes, as well as the ethics of Christianity, Islam or modernity, can easily be brushed aside when they conflict with kinship values and interests. The ethical structures created by modern African states and those created by Christianity and Islam seem not to moderate the behaviour, attitudes and practices of individuals or groups.

Biblical Christianity has to transform this traditional law of kinship with a Christian concept of a messianic community and Christian communitarian ethics that transcend ethnic or racial boundaries.

The place of outsiders and strangers

Anything outside of the kinship system is labelled as part of the "outside world" and as such is not owned by any human group. This label may be applied to governments, institutions, denominations and companies. They are seen as neutral ground, where kinship or tribal rules do not apply. In fact, there are no set rules to govern the operation or control of these institutions. To many Africans, however, these places are more battlefields than neutral ground. Within them, might is right and the end justifies the means. They are seen as territory waiting to be claimed by whoever is strong enough to do so. Thus they are full of war, rivalry, competition, intrigues, manipulation and stratagems.

When the colonial powers created new states in Africa, the institutions they set up were usually seen as part of the outside world. They were available as spoil or booty to whichever ethnic or tribal group could gain dominance or control by force or any other means. In colonial governments and institutions, ethnic groups or tribes saw themselves as competitors or warriors. The goal was to be dominant in order to get as much as you could for the sake of your kinship group.

Those other groups were to be subjugated and treated as outsiders. The only way in which they could gain respect was through hard means, such as war and conflict. The weak were expected to recognize and respect the dominance of the strong. As subjects, they were treated according to a different set of rules from the strong.

Not surprisingly, the result of these attitudes had been that ethnic or racial values have dominated the post-colonial governments of African states. They are rife with discrimination and preferential treatment. There is a drive to exclude others from political participation and representation. The fear of political and economic power or dominance has often led to tensions and conflicts, which are aggravated by modern political, economic, cultural, religious and social factors.

Biblical teachings on outsiders and strangers

The Bible repeatedly addresses the question of how outsiders or strangers are to be treated. In the Old Testament, the Israelites were commanded to treat strangers well because they, too, had been strangers in Egypt. They were not to make their experience of slavery and maltreatment in Egypt the norm for the way they treated others. They were to love foreigners (Lev 19:34); provide for them (Deut 10:18) and let them share the leftovers of the harvest (Deut 24:19–22).

The New Testament repeatedly stresses that the cross of Christ has created a new humanity, the messianic community, the church. Ethnicity, racism and tribalism have been abolished as all ethnic groups and races become one in Christ. The dividing wall of enmity that once separated

Jews and Gentiles has been abolished through the cross of Christ (Eph 2:14–17).

In Christ Jesus, no human being is to suffer discrimination or hostility from others. We must not discriminate against our Christian brothers and sisters, and we are called to love those who are our enemies (Matt 5:43–48).

Sin, Shame and Guilt in Africa

Traditional African thinking about sin, shame and guilt affects social and communal attitudes, behaviour and practice, and thus also affects social and communal sins.

The concept of sin in traditional Africa is probably best addressed in terms of the example of what it means to touch a forbidden thing. Doing so brings evil consequence for the person or group involved, and some ritual or sacrifice is needed to avert these consequences. Communal punishment will be meted out if the sin is seen or discovered. The understanding of sin here is similar to that which prevailed in relation to Achan in the Bible. He took forbidden things and was found out by casting lots. He and his entire family were killed and everything of theirs burnt (Josh 7:1–26).

Shame is felt by a person who touched the forbidden thing, and may also be felt by their household and their people. It is a discovery or an awareness that one is in a state of wrong. Thus shame is a state and not an act.

Guilt, on the other hand, defines an act as a transgression or breaking the law. Guilt is incurred by doing something wrong and is objective, whereas shame is a subjective experience. If someone does not realize that what they have done is wrong, or is certain that their wrongdoing has not been exposed, they may feel no shame. That is why our response to shame is to try to cover it in order to hide our nakedness or exposure. But guilt is incurred whenever we transgress a moral code. We have broken a law, and there are defined consequences for the offence. We will be punished for breaking the law.

African traditional societies did not have written moral or legal codes, but they did have taboos, customs and traditions that served as moral codes. Generally, these societies were law-abiding, because breaking traditional laws drew severe punishment, including death or banishment. There are few rebels in society. Certainly, traditional Africans knew when the laws had been broken and they also knew the judgements that would follow. They were thus familiar with guilt, the awareness that one has transgressed some law.

However, this guilt was understood in terms of an offence against the community, rather than as an offence against God. In terms of African Traditional Religion

> guilt is not an offence against a holy God who does not and cannot tolerate sin. Sin has no effect on God. There is no objective standard, so there is no question of transgressing his law. Man alone is the loser when he sins and yet if he can find and perform the right ritual, he can circumvent all the consequences of his sin.[88]

African society is rightly described as a "shame" society more than it is a "guilt" society. In other words, it is a society in which shame is far more powerful than guilt. What is meant by this is that even if an act is not a transgression in the eyes of the one committing it (in other words, he or she has no inner moral principle that judges the behaviour), the person will still experience shame because in the eyes of the community a forbidden thing has been touched. It is the community that is sinned against. Shame is community-induced and rises from the communal moral conscience. The person who has transgressed feels shame at having been seen or caught, but may not necessarily feel guilt.

How is morality to be measured in this type of moral context, where there seem to be no fixed moral standards? In African Traditional Religion,

> morality, goodness and virtue have no bearing on being a worthy practitioner of the faith. The most immoral person is totally capable of giving good religious counsel and performing the rituals required for positive spirit response. The key to wisdom is not the fear of God, but rather knowledge of the secrets, which spell out how to manipulate the spirit world successfully. One who has mastered these techniques and

proved to be successful is revered and honored, apart from moral and ethical considerations.[89]

The same applies when it comes to determining someone's spirituality.

> The efficacy of spirituality and the practice of rituals has nothing to do with the morality or ethics of the practitioner. Spirituality consists merely in knowing that the world is spirit-oriented and motivated, that man's whole existence is interpenetrated by these spirit beings and man can benefit from their services. Morality and ethics have nothing to do with these potentials. Spirits are amoral. Their response to man is capricious – either good or bad may issue from them. Spirit beings, be they ancestors or gods, respond to correct ritual, not to purity of heart or cleanness of hands. Likewise, the efficacy of rituals depends upon the correct performance of the act, with its proscription and not a right heart relationship.[90]

It is not that traditional Africans fail to understand wrong acts or evil deeds. They do understand them. They are also aware of the principle of punishment or retribution if laws are broken. However, there is always a religious ritual that can be used as a means of escape from punishment or to shield against any moral consequences.

This approach to moral issues explains why the focus in Africa falls on correct rituals and correct religious practice rather than goodness and virtue, or purity and holiness. Ethics is a matter of outward acts and not inner purity, motives or disposition.

If we grasp this point, we can understand how many African leaders can be very religious and yet commit all kinds of atrocities. They do not have a personal moral conscience or an awareness of guilt. They can find ways to excuse their crimes and atrocities. The pursuit of power is a far more important matter. So long as the right results are obtained, there is no need to worry about right moral behaviour or ethics.

Those Africans who are people of integrity, honesty, faithful and sincere, are usually scolded for refusing to do the needful thing for the tribe. In fact good people are usually rejected in politics for they are useless when it comes to amassing political and economic loot for their people. What counts in politics and economics is not moral integrity but influence and power.

This attitude is strengthened by the traditional African value of kinship, which means that sin, shame and guilt are felt by individuals or groups only in relationship to their kinship community and not in relationship to outsiders or strangers. The state is an outsider, and thus there is little sense of sin, shame or guilt with regard to actions involving the state. The state's moral and ethical codes are not morally binding because they come from the outside world and not from the kinship community.

The theological basis of this traditional morality is very different from Christian morality, which is based upon Scriptures and the revealed will of God. Christian morality teaches that our deeds are not to be separated from our motives. Both are judged by the Spirit of God and his word. It is not enough to carry out the right religious ritual – it must be done with godly motives and a pure inner disposition. God judges the heart and not just our outward acts and deeds (1 Sam 16:7).

Creating a Just, Participatory and Sustainable Society

Individualistic ethics and morality are very important, but we also need to work towards the creation of a moral society, moral institutions and a moral nation-state. Africa is crisis-ridden and chaotic, with a lack of human rights, peace, justice and equality. It is thus vitally important that we work to develop a just, participatory and sustainable society.[91] However, it is important to realize that

> moral advice and proclamation of moral ideals are insufficient. Only that which transcends morals, namely, the knowledge of the ultimate accountability of man and society to God and of the Grace of God by which men, being forgiven, forgive one another, can be the foundation of personal responsibility and responsible society.[92]

A responsible society is not an alternative to current social or political systems, but rather the criterion by which all existing social orders could be judged. It offers a standard to guide Christians when making specific choices with regard to combating social and communal sins and creating a climate for "social justice and the development of social conditions in which human dignity and freedom can find their expression as befits the nature and destiny of man as a child of God".[93] It is important to remember that "Christians are called to live responsibly, to live in response to God's act of redemption in Christ, in any society, even within the most unfavourable social structures."[94]

The creation of a participatory and sustainable society requires us to accept five theological conceptions:[95]

- moral accountability to God and neighbour
- the solidarity of the human family
- the sacred worth of each person and, hence, the primacy of equality over inequality
- historical freedom as a precondition of effective participation
- the reality of sin and, therefore, the need to control (limit) economic and political power.

These theological concepts centre round social and personal principles of ethics, but "the struggle for a just, participatory and sustainable society must also embrace a broader context: the relation between God, humanity and nature".[96] Humanity and nature belong within God's history with his creation in which justice and injustice, even life and death, are in conflict as a result of the fall. Modern Africa and the entire world stand the risk of being destroyed, as a result of a fallen relationship between God, humanity and nature. In order to save our earth's depleted resources we must develop a good ethical and moral approach to our society and the world.

Society (human relations) and ecosystems (non-human creation as humanity's home) are intimately interconnected and may not be separated, and so are justice and the sustainability of creation.[97] This biblical world view and the traditional African world view agree in being holistic.

The biblical mandate for humanity is: 1) the responsible dominion over the earth, that is, worldwide responsibility and stewardship in the face of the blatant misuse and exploitation of the world, its people and its resources; and 2) the struggle for "a just, participatory and sustainable society" through the expression of human solidarity and the understanding of neighbours as persons.[98] These theological moral concepts and insights provide principles for dealing with social and communal sins in Africa and the world.

Sustainability

Among the social and communal sins that affect human societies and even nature is our irresponsible stewardship of God's creation. Our present anxiety over global climate change stems from the fact that in our scramble for wealth, food and security we have created societies that are no longer sustainable societies:

> A sustainable society is one in which people live with each other and the physical environment in ways that lead to continuing life rather than destruction. In recent years much of the world has discovered that its present habits of consumption threaten the physical environment and the resources by which people themselves live. Humanity is one member of the ecosystem (also part of God's creation) and has to live in continuing interaction with it. Practices destructive of the ecosystem will also destroy human society. In this respect, justice characterized a human relationship with the whole ecosystem as well as the relationship with other human persons and groups.[99]

We therefore have "to make a deliberate transition to a sustainable global society in which science and technology will be mobilized to meet the basic physical and spiritual needs of people, to minimize human suffering and to create an environment which can sustain a decent quality of life for all".[100] In this sense, a focus on sustainability requires responsibility, justice and participation.

Justice

> A just society is the kind of society heralded by the prophets and Jesus in the words translated as "justice" and "righteousness". "Let justice roll down as waters" (Amos 5:24). "Seek first his kingdom and his justice (or righteousness)" (Matt 5:33). In a

> just society persons and groups (family, occupational, social, ethnic, national) relate to one another for the benefit of all. Persons and groups have the opportunity to become human in freedom and responsibility. We can give no single universal description of what truly human life is, for that is in part a function of cultural and social institutions. Yet we recognize a common humanity among all created in the image of God.[101]

In the name of righteousness the prophets of the Old Testament challenged the injustice of a society in which the poor went hungry and were exploited by the rich. We in Africa need to pay particular attention to this social understanding of righteousness and to how it relates to political and economic structures in our societies. We should also seek to vindicate the poor and the oppressed because the gospel of Christ leads Christians to a commitment to an equitable society in which every person has significance and dignity and where none is oppressed. We should work for the interests of others, even at the expense of our own interests or those of our community and should strive to reduce the gap between the rich and the poor. It is not enough just to confess these sins – that is how individual sins are handled. Social and communal sins must be addressed by working for social equity and social responsibility.

Participation

> A participatory society includes in the process of decision-making all those whom any decision affects. Decisions are thus made by people, with people, for people. The modes of participation are likely to vary in different societies and in different decisions within societies. But everywhere participation is concerned not merely with the making of decisions but also with the sharing of resources, both material and spiritual, and the sharing of the suffering and the benefits.[102]

We cannot solve social problems without establishing relationships between societies as well as between individuals. Such relationships must involve justice and participation. "As people become involved in making decisions in a society, they see the need for structural change at every level, especially when questions of development are involved."[103]

> Participation calls for a recognition of everybody's right to be consulted, to be heard and understood, whatever their political, economic or social status may be in society. Everyone must be involved in planning and action, giving as well as receiving. Participation means that each one take initiative in formulating or changing policies and becoming involved in directing their implementation.[104]

Application to Africa

The concepts we have been discussing in relation to a "responsible society" and "a just, participatory and sustainable society" were developed from global perspectives. We need to think about how they can be addressed to aspects of communal and social sins in modern Africa that contribute to a lack of justice, equality, freedom, participation and sustainability.

We can mention only a few of the historical social and communal sins that have haunted modern Africa. One was that the historical freedom of many ethnic groups was completely denied under colonialism. They were placed under the rule and political control of the most powerful ethnic groups and denied any political participation on their own. The basis of colonial socio-political structure was the primacy of inequality over equality. Thus, the social orders created by the colonial administrations in Africa were far from being just, participatory and sustainable. Instead, they were characterized by 1) differential treatment of ethnic groups or persons; 2) denial of political participation to some groups; 3) stratified inequality between ethnic groups or races; and 4) institutionalized socio-political, economic and religious structures of inequality. The continuity of the unjust colonial institutions in post-colonial Africa must be addressed from the perspective of the norms and goals of Christian social thought as outlined above. Justice, participation and sustainability are normative to the vision of the new social order in Africa that can deal effectively with communal and social sins.

Summary

Sin can be committed by individuals or by groups. In traditional Africa, punishment was meted out by the kinship community. Any wrong behaviour, attitude or practice required repentance either by the individual or by groups. The traditional acts of repentance and forgiveness were always accompanied by rituals or ceremonies. There were also rituals associated with establishing reconciliation and peace. This was always a public religious, moral and ethical activity.

In modern Africa, this traditional approach to dealing with social and communal sins no longer holds in most societies. The church has overemphasized an individualistic approach to sin and has neglected the communal approach to it. Yet the church is the new humanity, the messianic community, and is governed by Christ's new communitarian ethics and morality.

Besides preaching repentance and forgiveness of sins, whether of individuals or communities or tribes, we also need to address the modern African context by stressing Christian principles relating to justice, freedom, rights, equality, sustainability and participation. Structural sins that affect cultures, religions, economies, politics and societies, communities, institutions and nations must be addressed. Injustices, oppression, discrimination, biases, prejudices, corruption, conflict and violence are not just to be confessed but to be redressed and eradicated socially and structurally. What is needed is not only spiritual confession and repentance, forgiveness and reconciliation, but the setting up of structures and institutions to effect justice and peace.

Moral engineering alone is not enough as moralists have failed to transform African societies. Social engineering (in the areas of politics, economics and technology) alone is not enough as social engineers have failed to transform African societies. Both moral and social engineering are necessary and complementary.

What lies behind the world's systems are spirit powers that can only be dealt with by Christ's supreme power. Christian morality does not operate effectively within human minds, it needs complementary social institutions to strengthen, sustain and promote it. Christians do not operate in a spiritual vacuum but are in the world with all its spirit powers. For them to live and practice their faith freely, they also need social structures and social values that strengthen and reinforce their Christian faith. The Christianity of morally good Christians does not last beyond their generation. A Christianity that lasts is the one that renews and transforms humanity, societies, communities, tribes, races and nation-states.

18

CONCLUSION

Many Africans who have become Christians still have their traditional umbilical cords uncut. They are simply Christo-pagans. Their traditional morality and ethics have not been fully renewed and transformed by biblical teachings. They still live in bondage to sin and to spirit power, which separates them from their Maker. Their embrace of traditional morality also leads to communal and social sins that go against the biblical command to do justice and to love mercy.

One reason for the lack of transformation in their lives is that African Christians rely on popular opinions, traditional views and guesswork as their major sources when it comes to understanding and dealing with sin. The result is that their interpretations of sin fall short of God's holy standards and that few have victory over sin. That is why this book is important. It provides a comprehensive overview of scriptural teaching on the origin and roots of sin, clearly explaining the overlaps and the divergences between traditional thinking and Christian thinking.

The book also shows that God has provided a solution not only to the problem of sin in general but also to the three pairs of root sins that I call "the trinity of sin". The sins in each pair are different, and need different responses. All can be overcome by applying the power and the benefits of the cross of Christ to the sin problem we face as individuals and as communities, tribes and nations.

My prayer is that this book will have helped many Christians come to a better understanding of the sins with which they wrestle. I pray too that those who want to live a victorious Christ-like life with victory over sin will have found effective spiritual principles for dealing with sin, both personally and communally.

BIBLIOGRAPHY

Albrecht, P., ed. *Faith, Science and Future.* Minneapolis: Fortress, 1978.

Albrecht, P., ed. *Faith and Science in an Unjust World: Report of the World Council of Church's Conference on Faith, Science and the Future; vol. 2, Reports and Recommendations.* Minneapolis: Fortress, 1980.

Arruda, M., ed. *Ecumenism and a New World Order: The Failures of the 1970s and the Challenges of the 1980s.* Geneva: WCC, 1980.

Bounds, E. M. *Prayer and Spiritual Warfare.* New Kensington, Penn.: Whitaker House, 1984.

Buswell, J. O. *A Systematic Theology of the Christian Religion.* 2 vols. Grand Rapids: Zondervan, 1963.

Dulle, J. "What is the Nature of Sin?" www.onenesspentecostal.com/natureofsin.htm

Edwards, Jonathan. *The Religious Affections: A Christian's Character before God.* Edited by James M. Houston. Oregon: Multnomah, 1984.

Expository Dictionary of Bible Words. Edited by Stephen D. Renn. Peabody, Mont: Hendrickson, 2005.

Ferdinando, K. *The Triumph of Christ in African Perspective: A Study of Demonology and Redemption in the African Context.* Carlisle: Paternoster, 1999.

Ferguson, S. B. *The Holy Spirit: Contours of Christian Theology.* Downers Grove: Intervarsity, 1996.

Fleming, D. *Bridge Bible Directory.* Brisbane: Bridgeway, 1990.

Foster, R. J. and Smith, J. B. *Devotional Classics: Selected Readings for Individuals and Groups.* San Francisco: Harper, 1993.

Gilkey, L. *Maker of Heaven and Earth: The Christian Doctrine of Creation in the Light of Modern Knowledge.* Lanham, Md: University Press of America, 1959.

Grudem, W. *Systematic Theology: An Introduction to Biblical Theology*. Grand Rapids: Zondervan, 1994.

Idowu, E. B. *Olodumare: God in Yoruba Belief.* London: Longman, 1962.

Ikenga-Metuh, E. *Towards An African Theology of Man.* Unpublished paper, 1981.

Imbach, S. R. "Syncretism" in W. A. Elwell (ed.) *Evangelical Dictionary of Theology*. Carlisle: Paternoster, 1984.

Kato, B. H. "The Gospel, Cultural Context and Religious Syncretism", in J. D. Douglas (ed.) *Let the Earth Hear his Voice*. Minneapolis: Worldwide Publications, 1975.

Magesa, L. *African Religion: The Moral Traditions of Abundant Life*. Nairobi: Paulines, 1997.

Mbiti, J. S. *African Religions and Philosophy*. London: Heinemann, 1971.

Mbiti, J. S. *Introduction to African Religion*. London: Heinemann, 1975.

Mbiti, J. S. *The Prayers of African Religion*. London: SPCK, 1976.

Mbiti, J. S. *Prayer and Spirituality in African Religion*. Bedford Park: Australian Association for the Study of Religions, 1978.

Muelder, W. G. *Foundations of the Responsible Society*. New York: Abingdon, 1958.

Muelder, W. G. "A Just, Participatory and Sustainable World Society". *Nexus 59: Social Ethics Tradition* 23 (Summer 1980: 19–26), 1980.

Munby, D., ed. *World Development: Challenge to the Churches*. Washington: Corpus, 1969.

Murray, A. *The Power of the Blood of Jesus*. Repr. Grand Rapids: Zondervan, 1987.

Murray, John. *The Imputation of Adam's Sin*. Grand Rapids: Eerdmans, 1959.

Nabofa, M. Y. *The Significance of Blood in African Traditional Religion*. Unpublished paper, 1980.

Nee, W. *The Spiritual Man*. New York: Christian Fellowship Publishers, 1977.

Nee, W. *Questions on the Gospel*. Anaheim: Living Stream Ministry, 1992.

New Concise Bible Dictionary; edited by J. D. Williams. Leicester: Inter-Varsity, 1989.

NIV Compact Dictionary of the *Bible;* edited by J. D. Douglas and M. C. Tenney. Grand Rapids: Zondervan, 1989.

Nyirongo, L, *The Gods of Africa or The God of the Bible? The Snares of African Traditional Religion in Biblical Perspective*. Potchefstroom: IRS (series F2, no. 70), 1997.

Oji, E. D. *Ikpu Alu (Atonement) in Igbo Traditional Religion*. B.A. thesis: Jos: ECWA Theological Seminary, 1988.

Orr, J. *Sin as a Problem of Today*. London: Hodder & Stoughton, 1910.

Owen, J. *Sin and Temptation: The Challenge to Personal Holiness*. Repr. Portland, Ore: Multnomah, 1983.

Page, S. *Powers of Evil: A Biblical Study of Satan and Demons*. Grand Rapids: Baker, 1995.

Pascal, Blaise. *The Mind on Fire*. Repr. Portland: Multnomah, 1989.

Parrinder, G. *African Traditional Religion*. London: SPCK, 1962.

Seel, J. R. "Meet Your Neighborhood Neopagan". *Regeneration Quarterly* (Fall 1997).

Shorter, A. *Prayer in the Religious Traditions of Africa*. London: OUP, 1975.

Shorter, A. *Jesus and the Witchdoctor: An Approach to Healing and Wholeness*. Maryknoll: Orbis, 1985.

Steyne, P. M. *Gods of Power: A Study of the Beliefs and Practices of Animists*. Houston: Touch, 1990.

Steyne, P. M. *In Step with the Gods of the Nations: A Biblical Theology of Missions*. Houston: Touch, 1992.

The Open Bible. Expanded Edition; New King James Version. New York: Thomas Nelson, 1983.

Thielicke, H. *Theological Ethics: Foundations*. Grand Rapids: Eerdmans, 1966.

Thielicke, H. *Being Human ... Becoming Human*. Garden City, NY: Doubleday, 1984.

Thomas, I. D. E. *The Golden Treasury of Patristic Quotations From 50–750 AD*. Oklahoma City: Hearthstone, 1996.

Turaki, Y. *Tribal Gods of Africa; Ethnicity, Racism, Tribalism and the Gospel of Christ*. Jos, Nigeria: Cross Roads Communications, 1997.

Turaki, Y. *Christianity and African Gods: A Method in Theology*, 1999. IRS, Potchefstroom University.

Turaki, Y. *Foundations of African Traditional Religion and Worldview*. Nairobi: WordAlive, 2006.

Turaki, Y. *Ethical and Cultural Foundations of Nigerian Society*. Jos: National Institute for Policy and Strategic Studies (NIPSS), Nigeria, 2003.

Turaki, Y. *The Uniqueness of Jesus Christ*. Nairobi: WordAlive, 2006.

Turaki, Y. *African Christianity in Global Religious and Cultural Conflict*. World Evangelical Alliance (WEA) Theological Commission. Nairobi Evangelical Graduate School of Theology (NEGST), Sept. 20–24, 2006.

Turaki, Y. "The Techniques of African Pagan Spirituality" in Peter Jones (ed.), *On Global Wizardry: Techniques of Pagan Spirituality and a Christian Response*. Escondido, Cal.: Main Entry Editions, 2010.

Van der Walt, B. J. *Afrocentric or Eurocentric? Our Task in a Multicultural South Africa* (Series F2, no. 67). Potchefstroom, South Africa: IRS, 1997.

Webster, H. *Taboo: A Sociological Study*. New York: Octagon Books, 1973.

Webster's New Collegiate Dictionary, 1977.

Willard, Dallas. *Renovating the Heart: Putting on the Character of Christ*. Colorado Springs: Navpress, 2002.

Willmington, H. L. *Willmington's Guide to the Bible*, Wheaton: Tyndale House, 1984.

World Council of Churches *Statements of the World Council of Churches on Social Questions*. Geneva: Dept. on Church and Society, WCC, 1956.

NOTES

1. As Langdon Gilkey says, "Men had always felt bound by inward forces of evil, perverted from their true life by powers acting within themselves which were beyond their control" (*Maker of Heaven and Earth; the Christian Doctrine of Creation in the Light of Modern Knowledge* [Lanham, MD: University Press of America, 1959], 263. Blaise Pascal (1623–62) described sin as a "strange disorder" and an "inconsistency" (*Mind on Fire*. Edited by James Houston [Portland, Oregon: Multnomah Press, 1989), 51.
2. H. L. Willmington, *Willmington's Guide to the Bible* (Wheaton, Ill.: Tyndale House, 1984), 718. This is also in agreement with the definition of sin in the Westminster Shorter Catechism: "Sin is any want of conformity unto, or transgression of the law of God."
3. The ideas presented here are discussed at more length in my earlier book, *Foundations of African Traditional Religion and Worldview* (Nairobi: WordAlive, 2006).
4. B. H. Kato, *African Cultural Revolution and the Christian Faith* (Jos, Nigeria: Challenge, 1975), 36–41.
5. E. B. Idowu, *Olódùmarè: God in Yoruba Belief* (London: Longman, 1962); J. E. S. Mbiti, *Introduction to African Religion and Philosophy* (London: Heinemann, 1975).
6. L. Magesa, *African Religion: The Moral Traditions of Abundant Life* (Nairobi: Paulines, 1997).
7. P. M. Steyne, *Gods of Power: A Study of the Beliefs and Practices of Animists* (Houston: Touch, 1990).
8. Ibid., 58.
9. Ibid., 37.
10. Ibid., 60.
11. Ibid.
12. B. J. van der Walt, *Afrocentric or Eurocentric? Our Task in a Multicultural South Africa* (Series F2, no. 67; Potchefstroom, South Africa: IRS, 1997), 29–44.
13. Steyne, 64–65.
14. *Webster's New Collegiate Dictionary*, 1977.
15. *NIV Compact Dictionary of the Bible*.
16. H. L. Willmington, *Willmington's Guide to the Bible* (Wheaton, Ill.: Tyndale House, 1984), 601.
17. Willmington, 602.
18. J. O. Buswell, *A Systematic Theology of the Christian Religion* (2 vols.; Grand Rapids: Zondervan, 1963), 67.
19. *Expository Dictionary of Bible Words*.
20. Willmington, 603.
21. *Expository Dictionary of Bible Words*.

22. Willmington, 48.
23. Gilkey, 44.
24. Ibid., 61.
25. L. Magesa, *African Religion: The Moral Traditions of Abundant Life* (Nairobi: Paulines, 1997), 165–188.
26. Gilkey, 49. The arguments in the section that follows are drawn from Gilkey, 215–228.
27. Gilkey, 209–210. The arguments in the section that draw heavily on Gilkey, 215–228.
28. Gilkey, 275.
29. "Man" is used here to refer to the human race, both male and female, which is how the Hebrew word *adam* is used in Genesis 1:27 and 5:1–2.
30. Jonathan Edwards, *A Treatise Concerning Religious Affections* (1754; repr. Portland, Ore: Multnomah, 1984), 91.
31. Wayne Grudem, *Systematic Theology: An Introduction to Biblical Theology* (Grand Rapids, Mich.: Zondervan, 1994), 442.
32. Helmut Thielecke sees the image of God in this fashion: 1) This image has been created by God, and is thus the standard of what human beings were intended to be before the fall. 2) This image lost its perfection at the fall and was corrupted by sin. 3) This image has been renewed by the incarnation, death and resurrection of Jesus Christ, who is the "New Man" or the Last Adam. *Theological Ethics: Foundations* (vol 1; Grand Rapids: Eerdmans, 1979), 147-194.
33. Grudem, 412.
34. Helmut Thielicke based his understanding of theological ethics on the understanding that Christian ethics are at best interim ethics, that is, ethics after the fall. See Helmut Thielicke, *Theological Ethics: Foundations* (vol. 1; Grand Rapids, Michigan: Eerdmans, 1979.
35. Owen, vii. Much of the analysis of temptation in this chapter is based on John Owen's *Sin and Temptation: The Challenge to Personal Holiness* (1658; repr. Portland, Ore.: Multnomah, 1983).
36. This analysis is strongly influenced by Grudem, p. 494–497.
37. Horatio Palmer, "Yield Not to Temptation", hymn composed in 1868.
38. For further discussion of this point, see Turaki, *Christianity and African Gods: A Method in Theology* (Potchefstroom: IRS, 1999), 220–224.
39. Emefie Ikenga-Metuh, *God and Man in African Religion: A Case Study of the Igbo of Nigeria* (London: Geoffrey Chapman, 1981) and *Towards an African Theology of Man* (Unpublished paper, 1981). Leonard Nyirongo identifies five elements in human nature, which overlap to some extent with those of Ikenga-Metuh, saying that a human being consists of (a) "shadow or "double', (b) ghost, (c) vital breath, (d) destiny or guardian spirit and (e) name" (*The Gods of Africa or the God of the Bible? The Snares of African Traditional Religion in Biblical Perspective* [Potchefstroom, IRS, 1977], 100.
40. Ikenga-Metuh comments, "Of course, different societies conceive of these principles and their relationship in different ways but the conception of man as a unit and a life-force in vital relationship with other life-forces in the universe is a characteristic feature." Comparative Studies of African Traditional Religions (Onitsha, Nigeria: IMICO, 1987), 181–195.
41. Ikenga-Metuh, Comparative Studies of African Traditional Religions, 6–7.
42. Magesa, 8.
43. Grudem, p. 476. I am indebted to Grudem for much of the material in this section.
44. Many of the ideas in the sections that follow are derived from Watchman Nee, *The Spiritual Man* (New York: Christian Fellowship Publishers, 1968). 21–54.
45. Dallas Willard, *Renovating the Heart: Putting on the Character of Christ* (Colorado Springs: NavPress, 2002), 33.
46. Edwards, 6.

47. Nee, 36; Willard, 32; Pascal, 53–63.
48. Willard, 35.
49. Although my primary source for my understanding of root sins is the Bible, I must also acknowledge my debt to Langdon Gilkey (228–234) for his definitions of the self, anxiety and fear, and sin and evil.
50. John Chrysostom, as quoted in I. D. E. Thomas, *The Golden Treasury of Patristic Quotations from 50–750 AD* (Oklahoma City: Hearthstone, 1996).
51. The words translated "pride" in these contexts are derived from the root *ga'ah*, and include, *ge, ge'eh, ge'ah, ga'awah, ga'on'*.
52. Words derived from the root word, *zid* include *zed, zud* and *zadon*.
53. These words are derived from the root *gabah*.
54. Other words that are used for pride and arrogance include, *hyperephania* (Mark 7:22) and *hyperephanos* (Luke 1:51; 2 Tim 3:2; Jas 4:6; 1 Pet 5:5; Rom 1:30).
55. Gilkey, 144.
56. John Owen, *Sin and Temptation*, 9.
57. Ibid. 10–11.
58. Ibid.
59. Ibid.
60. Ibid.
61. The ideas in this section are based on Nee, 69–132.
62. The word translated "flesh" is *basar* in Hebrew and *sarx* in Greek.
63. Ibid., 70–71.
64. *The Penguin Guide to Synonyms and Related Words,* 2nd ed. (London: Penguin Books, 1994), 223.
65. The Hebrew words used for fear are the *yareh* group, which conveys all the meanings of fear. The words *gur* and *megorah* are better translated as "terror". *Pahad* and its derivatives are synonyms for *yareh*. This group of words suggests both the presence of a feared object and the trembling that that presence causes. The Greek words translated "fear" are similar to those of the Old Testament. *Phobos* (noun) and *phobeomai* (verb) indicate fear, terror, fright, or reverence; and *deilos* has the idea of dread.
66. Gilkey, 6.
67. Owen, 80.
68. Gilkey, 244.
69. This chapter is influenced by the thinking of Watchman Nee, *Questions on the Gospel* (Anaheim, California: Living Stream Ministry, 1992), 29–36.
70. Willmington, 760.
71. The following verses refer to *zoe*: John 3:14–16; 5:21; 6:35, 51; 10:10; 11:25; 12:25; 14:6, 9.
72. Grudem, 746.
73. Ibid.
74. Gilkey, 6.
75. Edwards, 89–93.
76. This section is heavily influenced by Vine, 235–236.
77. This section is derived from *The Open Bible: Expanded Edition,* NKJV, 1983, 412.
78. Gilkey, 240-246.
79. John Seel Jr., "Meet Your Neighborhood Neopagan". *Regeneration Quarterly,* Fall 1997; vol. 3, No 4.
80. Vine, 243.
81. Gehman, 231.
82. Steyne, 182–200.
83. Adeyemo, 1979, quoted in Gehman, 133.

84. S. R. Imbach, "Syncretism" in W. A. Elwell, *Evangelical Dictionary of Theology*, 1062.
85. *New Concise Bible Dictionary*, 129.
86. Ibid.
87. D. Fleming, *Bridge Bible Directory* (Brisbane: Bridgeway, 1990), 271.
88. Steyne, 309.
89. Ibid.
90. Ibid.
91. This section draws on and modifies the ideas presented in chapter six of my dissertation, Yusufu Turaki, "Towards a Conception of a Just, Participatory and Sustainable Society", in "The Institutionalization of the Inferior Status and Socio-Political Role of the Non-Muslim Groups in the Colonial Hierarchical Structure of the Northern Region of Nigeria: A Socio-Ethical Analysis of the Colonial Legacy." Ph.D. Dissertation, Boston University, 1982.
92. Statements of the World Council of Churches on Social Questions, 26.
93. Ibid., 33.
94. Ibid., 49.
95. W. G. Muelder, "A Just, Participatory and Sustainable World Society", *Nexus 59: Social Ethics Tradition* 23 (Summer 1980), 19.
96. P. Albrecht, ed. *Faith, Science and the Future*. (Minneapolis: Fortress Press, 1978).
97. Ibid., 32.
98. Ibid., 36–37.
99. Albrecht, *Faith and Science in an Unjust World: Report of the World Council of Church's Conference on Faith, Science and the Future; vol. 2, Reports and Recommendations* (Minneapolis: Fortress, 1980), 92.
100. Ibid.
101. Ibid., 148.
102. Ibid., 148.
103. M. Arruda, *Ecumenism and a New World Order: The Failures of the 1970s and the Challenges of the 1980s* (Geneva: WCC, 1980), 13.
104. Ibid.

www.ingramcontent.com/pod-product-compliance
Lightning Source LLC
Chambersburg PA
CBHW070648160426
43194CB00009B/1629